THE SHOP FOR
THE PEOPLE

Two Centuries of Co-operative
Enterprise in Hull and East Yorkshire

by
John E. Smith

Hutton Press
1998

Published by
The Hutton Press Ltd.,
130 Canada Drive, Cherry Burton,
Beverley, East Yorkshire HU17 7SB

Copyright © 1998

Front Cover Picture Top:
The Hull Co-op Grocery and Butchery branches in Grovehill Road, Beverley, pictured in the 1930s.

Front Cover Picture Bottom:
The first of many electric mobile shops was built for the Hull Co-op by A.E. Morrison & Sons of Leicester in 1939. Based at Marfleet Grocery branch, it served the East Hull housing estate.

Back Cover Picture
The pre-war Central Premises of the Hull Co-operative Society in Jameson Street, Hull.

ISBN 1 902709 00 4

Printed and bound by
Fretwells Ltd., Hull.

CONTENTS

AUTHOR'S NOTE

Having been active for some time in the local Co-operative Movement, I felt something ought to be done in the 1990s to mark the first two hundred years of Co-operative trading in Hull and the East Riding. After all, the Co-op seems to have touched the lives of so many people over the years. Encouraged by the interest shown in my talks on *More than Divi and Milk Checks* (I've now given over 100 of these, after mistakenly thinking they would peter out after about half a dozen), I began the daunting task of turning nearly 30 years of research into something resembling a book.

The end result is not the usual rags-to-riches tale of some family firm in which a Victorian self-made businessman and his descendants figure large; it is a story of the People's Business - the Co-operative. It is therefore fitting that many have co-operated to put it together.

Special tribute must be paid to the late Mr. Samuel Marshall JP FCIS FLAA whose own book - published in 1951 - inspired my interest, and later involvement, in the Co-operative Movement. Discovering it by chance one day while browsing the shelves of Hull's Central Library, I quickly became captivated by his account of the vision and persistence of the city's Co-operative pioneers in the face of many difficulties. I have drawn extensively upon his work and can only hope he would have approved of my attempts to update his research.

I am most grateful to all those members and employees of the Hull and East Riding Co-operative Society who were kind enough to share with me their amazing memories. Their capacity to recall minute details of long-past events and their enduring devotion to the Co-operative cause both fascinated and impressed me. More than once it was said, 'You could fill an entire book with the happenings of every Department.' Sadly, much material and many anecdotes have had to be left out,

although some may now be added to the Co-operative archives at the University of Hull, for the benefit of generations to come.

I would also like to thank everyone who has lent me photographs and supplied invaluable technical assistance.

My sincere appreciation then, to: Joan Badham, Edna Beckett, Joyce Bellamy, Mrs E. Blackburn, Bob and Rita Border, T.W. Bourne, Alfred Brough, Ian Campbell, Eric Cant, Frederick Cant, Ruth Clarke, Stan Clixby, Sheila Coates, Charles Collinson, Joyce Cook, Ernest Cooper, Mrs Cooper, John Cottis, Bob Crowe, Don Culpan, Herbert Day, Ken Dearing, Frank Dent, Andrew Dinkenor, Mrs Duffill (née Sainsbury), Mrs Eastwood, Joyce Eaton (née Lewis), Mrs Elvin, Doris Farmery (née Compston), Edgar Featherstone, Gordon Foster, Mary Fowler, Jean Frisby (née Limon), Cyril Gardham, Rena Gordon (née Wragg), Lilian Goring, Rita Green, Mrs M. Greenwood, Roy Gregory, Mrs M. Groves, Leslie Harling, Cyril Harrison, Mary Hellings, Frank Henderson, Mrs Hind, Emily Hodgson, Bernard Howcroft, Pat and Mrs Howlett, Mrs Jackson, Ron Jaques, Kenneth Kaye, Chris Ketchell, Mike Kemp, Reginald Kemp, Jack King, Reg Lamb, Hilary Lawn, Ron Lazenby, Gillian Lonergan, Stan Lummiss, Andrew McVeigh, Barbara Magee (née Kitching), Bob Mair, Mike Mathieson, Philip Meldrum, Arthur and Dorothy Moore, John Morfin, Jean Oxley, Charles Pearson, Geoff Percival, Harry Plaxton, Jean Poskitt, Len Pounder, Dorothy Ramsey, Tony Rippon, John Roberts, Brian Robinson, Pat Robinson, Betty Russell, Clarice Scruton, Nellie Senior, Malcolm Shields, Janet Slater, Ben Smelt, Angela Smith, Flo Smith, Horace Smith, Ken Smith, Ron Smith, Mrs J.E. Stockhill, Kathleen Thompson, Leslie Walker, Sandra Walker, Les Ward, Peter Ward (Comfy Products), Bruce Warnes, Doug Widdowson, Herbert and Mrs Williamson, Julie Withell, Andy Woodburn, CRS, CWS, CIS, Co-operative Bank, Co-operative Union, Kingston upon Hull City

Archivist, City Museums and Local Studies Library, Registry of Friendly Societies, Innes Studios (Hessle), Richmond & Rigg, The University of Hull.

Keeping track of every source of information has not been easy and so I apologise if anyone has been missed.

Most of my book is devoted to the development of the region's largest society, the Hull Co-operative Society. However, it also describes some of the other Co-ops in East Yorkshire, an area with a long and proud Co-operative tradition. It is a story of ups and downs; of triumphs and setbacks; of ordinary folk meeting - and overcoming - hostility and obstacles, in their struggle to make life a little better for themselves and their fellow human beings. It is to all those people - members of the great Co-operative Family, past, present and future - that it is lovingly dedicated.

John E. Smith
September 1998.

'The Shop for the People' is the proud claim in this 1930 view of the Co-operative Stores at the corner of Spring Bank West and Calvert Lane, Hull.

INTRODUCTION

Nearly everyone seems to have heard of The Co-op. Mention it in older company and you'll evoke instant recall of Mother's share number, standing in a queue to collect 'the divi', or perhaps saving up CWS Soap wrappers to exchange for free towels. Among the younger generation too there's often a surprising awareness of Co-operatives and their long history of ethical and environmental campaigning.

Years ago, with shops in every town (and many villages too), local Co-operative Societies played a big part in everyday life. As likely as not it was Co-op delivery people who brought the milk, the coal and the groceries to our door, and the Co-op Insurance Man whose regular visits helped us cope with life's troubles. And most of us knew someone who either worked for the Co-op or was somehow involved in its Guilds, choirs or committees.

To discover the Co-op's roots, however, we have to go back to the early 1800s - a time when the Industrial Revolution was changing the face of Britain. While the new factory owners prospered, the workers were finding it hard to make ends meet. Their plight was made even worse when the local shopkeepers gave short measure and charged extortionate prices for poor quality goods. It was clear that something had to be done.

The new political movements and the Free Churches gave many ordinary people the confidence to fight for a better life. And the ideals of social reformers like Robert Owen, coupled with the Victorian ethos of self-help, inspired them to co-operate to obtain their material needs. Many of these early attempts failed but in 1844, by scraping together a meagre capital of £28 to open a tiny store in Toad Lane, Rochdale, 28 working men managed to found a consumers' movement that was to revolutionise shopping for years to come.

By 1900 the Rochdale model had proved so attractive that some 1,400 Co-op retail societies had sprung up across Britain to cater for the members who owned and ran them. Unlike company-run chain stores they all operated independently. But together they ranked as one of the greatest mass membership organisations of all time. They succeeded by adhering to a set of well thought out principles and working practices:
- open and voluntary membership;
- an equal say for all (one member, one vote);
- limited interest on share capital;
- profit sharing according to each member's loyalty (the famous Co-op dividend);
- pure foods and honest weights and measures; and
- educational opportunities for their members and workers.

For millions of Co-op members, the incentive of the dividend (which put cash into the pockets of ordinary shoppers instead of wealthy businessmen) turned shopping there into a deeply ingrained way of life. Indeed, for some, supporting their society almost took on a religious fervour. There were those who wouldn't have been seen dead inside a private enterprise shop; they would sooner go without what the Co-op hadn't got than darken the doors of its rivals. Similar loyalty extended to Co-operatively-produced goods. Members would resolutely insist on 'CWS' (or a myriad Co-op brand names like Wheatsheaf and Pelaw) to support the factories that their own savings had helped to build; factories where it was axiomatic that things were made to last, and the workers enjoyed exemplary conditions of labour.

Soon people were forming workers' co-ops and applying the principles to agriculture, fisheries, housing and financial services. And the idea spread overseas, until today there are more than 760 million co-operators in no fewer than 90 countries of the world.

In our more affluent age, The Co-op may be less central to our lives, but collectively it still represents one of Britain's largest and most diverse businesses. What is more, after years of seeing more selfish motives promoted as the recipe for success in life, Co-operation as a philosophy seems to be coming back into fashion. People are discovering in all sorts of ways that working together democratically is a good way of improving community life. They are busy running playgroups; taking part in home-care projects; getting involved in Neighbourhood Watch; organising credit unions; forming bulk-buy clubs and local exchange schemes, and so on. Common to all these is the coming together of people from all walks of life to develop the capacity to do things for themselves rather than have them 'handed down' by well-meaning professionals. Whether they realise it or not, such ventures are co-operatives in all but name. Who knows what others will spring up to meet our future needs? At the time of writing there are even plans to set up a new supporters' forum for Hull City Football Club, owned and run by the fans themselves, called 'Tigers Co-operative'.

For the established Co-op Movement, progress on the trading front has been matched by signs of a revival of member interest. A national recruitment drive styled 'You make the difference' recently brought 100,000 new members into one of our largest retail Co-ops - CRS. An encouraging number are starting to take an active interest in the Society, as anyone who has attended a Humberside CRS Members' Meeting will have seen for themselves. With its high profile ethical stance the Co-operative Bank too has gained many converts (particularly among the environmentally - conscious young), stealing a march on its rivals by placing Co-operative values at the very heart of all its dealings.

As we approach a new millennium, those very values - self-help through mutuality, democracy, fairness, honesty, openness and caring for others - may yet inspire a whole new generation in their quest for a happier, kinder and more sustainable world.

Advertising snippets illustrating the wide range of services provided by the Hull Co-op in the 1930s.

CHAPTER ONE - 'LET'S START WITH A FLOUR MILL' 1795-1890

The Rochdale Pioneers of 1844 are rightly celebrated as the founders of the world's first successful Co-operative Society. However, the idea of a business run by the people for the people, and motivated by service rather than profit, goes back much further than that. Indeed the very notion of 'co-operation' - working together for a common purpose - is as old as civilisation itself.

In Kingston upon Hull, a consumers' co-operative came into being some fifty years before Rochdale. It was a time of unbearable misery for the townsfolk, whose numbers during the final quarter of the 18th century had doubled to nearly 30,000. Food was already scarce, mainly as a consequence of the French wars. But when a run of disastrous harvests caused a sharp rise in the price of flour, there were many on the point of starvation.

Convinced that the local millers and bakers were profiteering from their misfortune, some of the angry populace took to rioting, and a wave of property-breaking swept through the town. Those in authority showed no sympathy, however. Instead of organising help for the afflicted, they swiftly called in the militia to quell the irate mob.

Fortunately one small group of individuals came up with a far more enlightened idea. They devised an ingenious plan to build themselves a mill which, being under their own control, would guarantee them supplies of quality, low-cost flour. To progress their vision they invited subscriptions of '1s. 1d. per week for four weeks and 6d. per week for four weeks more' (a total of 6s. 4d or 32p each) from anyone willing to become involved. With a little financial help from the Mayor and Aldermen of the town and a few other sympathisers, a society known as the HULL ANTI-MILL INDUSTRIAL SOCIETY was formed on 24th September 1795 and soon had 1,435 members on its books.

It was Sir Henry Etherington, one of the benefactors, who laid the foundation stone for the enterprise, on the Holderness Road, on 7th June 1796. The five-sail windmill cost upwards of £2,200 to build and its official opening, one year later to the day, was celebrated in grand style. According to the *English Chronicle*, the band of the Durham Militia led a procession to the Market Place and marched three times around the King William statue playing *God Save the King*. The founders then proceeded to the mill for an elegant dinner, after which they toasted its success with two crown bowls of punch, 'amidst a great deal of hilarity and rejoicing.'

Over the next fifty years the Anti-Mill went from strength to strength. In 1847 a new share issue increased its membership to 2,500 and made it possible to introduce steam power. That the Society was barely profitable merely reflected its deliberate policy of selling flour as near cost as possible. But when money did start to be made, in 1855, the members received a cash bonus of 3½d. a stone; this was, in effect, their first Co-op dividend. Until then the Society had traded exclusively with its members but, following an amendment to the rules, flour was also distributed to the general public through about 20 local shops.

It seems the very poor couldn't afford the Anti-Mill subscription of 6/4d. and so in 1800 another society was formed to erect a cheaper mill in Dansom Lane. Known as the HULL SUBSCRIPTION MILL, it attracted 2,000 members and capital of £3,567.

Selling their flour for considerably less than the four shillings a stone charged by the private millers, both mills were a godsend for the poor. Another blessing was the quality of their product. In those days flour was often adulterated with china clay, causing it to weigh heavier in order to inflate the trader's profit margin. The Co-operative mills, having no incentive to cheat their own members, sold only the purest bread-making flour.

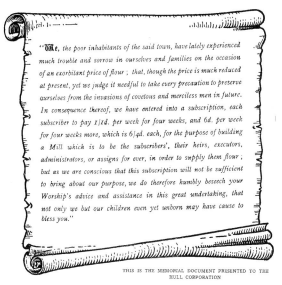

*"**We**, the poor inhabitants of the said town, have lately experienced much trouble and sorrow in ourselves and families on the occasion of an exorbitant price of flour; that, though the price is much reduced at present, yet we judge it needful to take every precaution to preserve ourselves from the invasions of covetous and merciless men in future. In consequence thereof, we have entered into a subscription, each subscriber to pay 1/1d. per week for four weeks, and 6d. per week for four weeks more, which is 6/4d. each, for the purpose of building a Mill which is to be the subscribers', their heirs, executors, administrators, or assigns for ever, in order to supply them flour; but as we are conscious that this subscription will not be sufficient to bring about our purpose, we do therefore humbly beseech your Worship's advice and assistance in this great undertaking, that not only we but our children even yet unborn may have cause to bless you."*

THIS IS THE MEMORIAL DOCUMENT PRESENTED TO THE HULL CORPORATION

With so much poverty locally, the funds pledged to the Anti-mill fell far short of requirements. The promoters therefore presented this petition to the Hull Corporation humbly appealing for aid.

Hull Subscription Mill

Hull Subscription Mill Member's Pass Card. The Brasso factory of Reckitt & Sons was later built on the site of this mill (Local History Unit postcard).

'Headquarters' of the Hull Co-operative Provident Company in Lowgate, then one of Hull's principal shopping thoroughfares.

The Anti-Mill clearly posed a threat to Hull's private millers, for they sought to indict it as a nuisance at York Assizes on 1st August 1811. However, the Yorkshire jurors were decidedly unimpressed by its opponents. Believing poverty to be a far greater nuisance, they found in its favour.

After nearly a century of usefulness to the people of Hull, both mills were in serious decline by the late 1880s. With the advent of roller milling and other developments the industry was undergoing a technological revolution. The societies' members were unwilling (or more likely, unable) to invest the extra capital necessary to allow their mills to keep pace. From a peak of £13,500 the Subscription Mill's sales plummeted to £3,650 by 1888. The profits also shrank to £38, foreshadowing its demise two years later. On winding up, members were set to receive around 12 shillings a share but many had long since given it up as a bad job and burned their cards. After achieving record sales of £77,569 in 1877, the Anti-Mill too steadily declined, finally fading from the scene in 1897. Among its many managers had been Slater Eyre, a relation of Hull's celebrated milling magnate, Joseph Rank.

At least three other Co-operative mills have existed in East Yorkshire. An anti-monopoly mill on the Gypsey Race at BRIDLINGTON was first recorded in 1793; another was erected at GILBERDYKE around 1800, while on Beverley Westwood the remains of the BEVERLEY UNION MILL (established in 1799) were later converted into a club-house for the town's golf course.

The first attempt to open a general-purpose Co-operative Store in Hull came around 1857 with the establishment of the HULL CO-OPERATIVE PROVIDENT COMPANY (LIMITED). Though registered as a company, it exhibited several features of the Rochdale pattern of trading, including the dividend on purchases. Metal tokens were issued with every purchase and members had to keep exchanging their shillings and pence tokens for pound ones, which were then handed back to the Store each quarter-end to claim the dividend.

Anxious to promote education, the Company set up a Reading Room next to its Central Stores at 2 Dock Street. By 1860 sales were averaging £70 a week and the dividend was 1/- in the £. But with so many Hull families living below the poverty line, trade was painfully slow to develop. Eventually 'Central' was removed to 57 Lowgate and branches were established at Cumberland Street; Eastgate, Beverley; Dairycoates (where the North Eastern Railway Company had a large locomotive works); and, strangely enough, a distant outpost at Saxby in Lincolnshire.

Groceries, Boots and Shoes, Crockery and Coal were sold and there was a Life Assurance agency. It appears the Company pioneered the employees' weekly half-day holiday and even pushed the sale of a national publication, *The Co-operator*. In 1865, in an early show of co-operation between Co-operatives, it joined forces with the two Mills to organise a Co-operative Trip to Hornsea along the newly-opened railway line. Plans were also hatched for yet another mill - the HULL UNITED FLOUR MILL AND INDUSTRIAL SOCIETY - to supply the Provident Company with flour. This short-lived venture got off to a somewhat shaky start in 1866, for during its first year the Mill stood idle for an average of three days a week for want of wind!

Despite Provident Company propaganda claiming that the dividend was equivalent to a month's free groceries, loyalty was waning by 1880. Members were warned that if they continued to trade elsewhere they would lose both the Company and their money. The sudden withdrawal of the debenture stock in 1882 was the final straw, forcing the business into liquidation. Members received just 13/10d. for each £1 share. The Secretary, Mr. John Toyn Upton, went on to form a local building society called The Lion but this too eventually failed.

CHAPTER TWO - LAYING THE FOUNDATIONS 1890-1900

By the late 19th century Kingston upon Hull had a population of 200,000 and was still growing; it had become the tenth largest town in England. Its workers toiled mainly in the busy Port, and in the great seed-crushing, sawmilling and shipbuilding industries associated with it. The majority of its inhabitants made their homes in the streets of tightly-packed terraces that had sprung up along each of the main roads radiating from its town centre. And yet, for all its size and importance, Hull - unlike most other Northern towns - still lacked a thriving retail Co-operative Society.

Indeed, the collapse of the Provident Stores and imminent demise of the original consumer-owned flour mills seemed to spell the end of Hull's Co-operative adventure. But it was mainly commercial pressure, rather than waning enthusiasm for the cause, that had defeated these pioneering projects. Those involved doubtless regarded it as a setback, but men of such faith and tenacity were unlikely to give up so easily. For one thing, they had some highly influential friends. The Hull Trades Council - a trade unionist body with a strong voice in local politics - was now in the ascendancy. Its members saw the Co-operative Movement as a powerful ally in the working-class struggle against poverty, unemployment, bad housing and poor diet.

The notion of re-launching the 'People's Stores' on a sounder footing was aired at a meeting in the Foresters' Hall, Charlotte Street, Hull on 19th December 1889. The impetus for this had come from a Mr. Ballan Stead, the Secretary of the Ancient Order of Foresters Friendly Society, but a group of shipwrights from the Earle's Shipyard on Hedon Road also backed the idea. A Propaganda Committee was duly formed to plan further meetings in various districts in order to drum up popular support.

The last of these took place in the Ripon Hall, Holderness Road on 14th January 1890, and was presided over by a respected local industrialist,

Alderman James Stuart JP. Recalling the achievements of the Anti-Mill a century before, Ald. Stuart urged his audience to give the proposal their full support. Despite a number of passionate speeches, however, it seems not everyone was impressed. According to the *Eastern Morning News*, a shopkeeper called Laikin leapt out of his seat at one point and defied Co-operative Stores 'to supply either groceries, drapery, drugs, furniture ... or boots and shoes cheaper than they can be got on the Holderness Road'. But the general mood was clearly one of 'let's have a go', for a motion proposing that a Society be formed was voted upon and carried with only six dissenters.

At the inaugural General Meeting of the KINGSTON UPON HULL CO-OPERATIVE SOCIETY LTD. in April 1890 the first officers were elected: President: Councillor W.G. Millington; Secretary: Mr. W.H. Taylor; Treasurer: Mr. Thomas Seymour; Management Committee: Messrs. T.B. Stead, T.C. Taylor, C. Moulds, J.M. James, W.J. Payling, M. Taylor, W.H. Butterfield and J. Fulcher. Pressure of business, however, soon forced Cllr. Millington to step down in favour of Mr. James.

The Committee planned to begin operations with two shops - one on either side of the River Hull. In the meantime, officers were in attendance at the Foresters' Hall on Monday evenings and visited the local Trade Union branches to sign up members and accept their share contributions. However, initial caution on the part of the working people of Hull caused deposits to fall far short of what was needed to go into business. The Co-operative Wholesale Society (CWS) finally saved the day by offering a loan of £250, at 5% interest, the same rate as the Society planned to offer its members. The loan took six years to pay off and when it was settled a Tea Party was given to celebrate!

After an exhaustive search, shop premises were rented at 201 Hessle Road (Wassand Street corner) for £38 a year, and trading began on

The Hull's Co-op's Wilton Terrace Grocery store (later known as 27 Holderness Road). At the door are Messrs. Hord, Honor, Bentley and Pashby (Lord Mayor of Hull 1938-9) (Picture by courtesy of Mrs B. Russell).

Mr John Mansell James, one of the founders of the Kingston upon Hull Co-operative Society Ltd. He held office as President, then Secretary, and later as Cashier.

Some of the Society's activists in 1900 who organised a Grand Exhibition of Co-operative Productions in the Assembly Rooms, Kingston Square, to commemorate its first ten years.

Saturday, 14th June 1890. The opening day's takings came to £14/5/2d and 104 members had enrolled, investing some £200 in share capital. By the end of the first week, sales had reached £41. Regarding this as a promising start, the Committee organised a Public Tea Meeting at the Sailors' Institute in Waterhouse Lane to celebrate the launch of their first store.

At the Tea Party the President confirmed they were still on the look-out for a shop in East Hull. Before long there was news of one coming on the market in Drypool. The location was ideal but the Committee promptly turned the premises down because they held a beer licence. Several of the Committee men were staunch teetotallers who felt that to supply alcoholic beverages would offend the true purpose of Co-operation. The issue was viewed with such gravity that a Special Meeting of the Society was called but, after careful deliberation, the members wholeheartedly endorsed their Committee's principled stance.

Soon a stream of correspondence began to appear in the daily Press. It came mainly from the local shopkeepers. What they had initially dismissed as 'amateur shopkeeping' suddenly seemed to pose a serious threat; they were anxious to persuade citizens to have nothing to do with it. Fortunately the Society had a marvellous champion in its President, John Mansell James. A shipwright of indomitable spirit, he handled the Co-operative side of the publicity with great aplomb. Quoting some impressive national Co-operative statistics, he invited the people of Hull to think it over; such figures didn't look to him like failure.

The Store opened each weekday at 8 am. and closed on Mondays to Wednesdays at 7 pm; Thursdays at 1 pm; Fridays at 8 pm; and Saturdays at 11 pm. These hours are more significant than might at first be thought, for they made the Co-op a pioneer of weekly half-day closing in Hull, as it was later in setting a minimum wage for shop assistants. The Society received a vote of thanks from the Shop Assistants' Trade Union for these progressive moves. The Store Manager's weekly wage in 1890 was 26 shillings and there was one Assistant on £1 a week.

On 14th September 1890 a second shop was opened at 11 Wilton Terrace, Holderness Road. For the first few years, the Society could only manage to retail Food and small articles of Hardware. To meet members' Non-food requirements, agencies were entered into with about a dozen private traders so that they could obtain dividend checks when patronising their businesses. These arrangements covered Drapery, Boots and Shoes, Hats and Caps, Tailoring, Readymade Clothing, Furniture and Coal.

Business methods were extremely primitive by comparison with those of today. For the first three months the President himself delivered goods to members living all over town with a handcart that the Society had bought for £2! Later, a pony and trap was hired three times a week for eight shillings. Branch managers were expected to rise especially early to visit the early morning market to buy potatoes. And butter and eggs were bought from the country wagoners' carts as they passed the Stores on their way to the Old Town markets. The idea was quite simple - to cut out the middleman and obtain as much produce as possible direct from the growers.

Just how meagre those purchases were may be gleaned from two sample Minute Book entries, one stipulating: 'That flour be purchased from a local mill at £3/12/6d.'; the other authorising the President 'to call upon a local wholesaler and endeavour to purchase about six nice hams and shoulders that the Society could sell at 4d. per pound'. It was truly a hand to mouth operation.

Despite being merely spare-time volunteers, the early Committee men involved themselves in all kinds of minor matters which were later delegated to paid employees. Thus, one of their number was responsible for entering up the Goods Received Book; another for keeping a detailed record of all wholesale and retail prices. Those involved gave hours of enthusiastic service for very little recognition or reward.

The possibility of failure constantly haunted the Society's leaders. Every penny was carefully watched; to keep down the wages bill, the Committee men would lend a hand in the Stores whenever the staff fell sick or required holidays. Each member's purchasing record was also regularly examined. Where loyalty appeared to be flagging, volunteers would visit them at home to ascertain why. Such members were granted only 2½% interest on their shares, half the rate enjoyed by the better spenders.

Although the Rochdale Pioneers had advocated cash-only trading, times were desperately hard for the workers of Hull, whose existing credit commitments kept them tied to the corner shops. To make it easier for them to move their custom to the Co-op, it was decided in October 1890 to allow members to buy on credit during the week provided they paid up by the following Saturday. No second order could be delivered until the first was settled. Even so, the whole concept was anathema to John Mansell James who never tired of counselling members to keep out of debt. The full fruits of Co-operation would never be realised, he contended, while credit prevailed.

Sales at Hessle Road declined and it was decided not to renew the lease when it expired on 9th May 1891. The task of delivering to the western side of town was taken on by the Management Committee until they could find a suitable strong boy. Before being allowed to take up this responsible position, the boy had to produce references from his schoolmaster, also from his previous employer, and appear before the full Committee for questioning! The wage offered was 10 shillings a week.

After just 15 months' trading, though the business had yet to show a profit, members were treated to their first dividend. The rate recommended by the Committee to the Members' Meeting was 6d. per £ of members' purchases, the sum provided in the accounts being £8/19/6d. To pay any dividend at all while making losses might seem a most unsound practice, but the Board felt it would give the workers of Hull confidence in the enterprise and attract many more to join. The tactic paid off handsomely. Once the word spread around that shoppers were getting cash back for trading with the Co-op, the Society never looked back. To celebrate this milestone, another Public Tea Party was held.

In 1894, with the business firmly established, it was decided to arrange a railway excursion for 400 members and their families to Manchester Zoo. The railway companies competed keenly for this contract, which was awarded to the Hull and Barnsley Railway Co. A special fast train ran out of Cannon Street station at 6 am., returning from Manchester at 11 pm. The return fare of 3/3d. included admission to the Belle Vue Pleasure Gardens and returned a profit to the Society of £2/12/6d. The Secretary even asked the General Manager of the Earle's Shipyard to give all the Co-op members who worked there a day off to take part and advance them their wages the day before!

A Boot Department was now opened, with a Miss Pexton in charge, this being the earliest record of female staff. The Coal business was also entered, the first rulleyman being a Mr. Newton. For Bespoke Clothing, a tailor came over from Manchester on certain evenings to see members by appointment. At other times one of the Grocers or the Secretary (Mr. James) would simply run the tape around the customer and forward the measurements on.

Like so many Victorian institutions, the Society was run exclusively by men at first. However, the need to enlist the support of the womenfolk

Original Central Premises at the corner of Jarratt Street and Charles Street, Hull. The Drapery and Boot departments moved across to Jameson Street in 1908; Furnishing in 1917.

Depot for washing, smoking and rolling bacon, Maple Street. The Co-op was keen to establish a good name in bacon; it was well-known in the trade that this was the way to turn casual customers into regulars.

was evidently realised at the April 1895 Members' Meeting, for it was resolved: 'That a Women's Guild be formed.' The Guild met at the Foresters' Hall on Tuesday evenings, its first President being a Mrs Horton. With the election of Mrs E. Edmond to the Board in 1900, the power of the 'woman with the shopping basket' would surely begin to make itself felt.

Later in 1895 an Educational Committee was also formed, comprising Messrs. W.J. Pond (Chairman), Thomas Penn (Secretary), Walter Horton, Walter Litchfield, J. Longden, Mesdames Rose, Evans and Lyons. If the Grocery Department's purpose was to sustain a Co-operator's physique, it fell to the Educational Department to nurture his or her mind - with literature, lectures and a variety of cultural and social experiences. A Mr. J.J. Harrison was appointed to teach the *History and Principles of Co-operation* and propaganda meetings were organised, in order to spread the 'gospel'. A Co-operators' Cycle Club and a Field Naturalists' Club enticed members away from their smoky, grimy streets into the open countryside. And long processions of wagonettes could often be seen ferrying excited youngsters down Holderness Road to a favourite field at Ganstead for a picnic.

Despite warnings from the CWS not to let their enthusiasm run away with them, the Board couldn't resist expanding into the Waterloo Street estate, an area heavily populated with mill and factory workers. The tenancy of a small shop was secured there in September 1895. As an experiment, an upstairs room was fitted out for the sale of Boots, Shoes, Hardware, Crockery, Readymade Clothing and Drapery. Just how it must have looked is best left to the imagination, but images of Aladdin's Cave spring readily to the writer's mind!

In 1896 the Society returned to Hessle Road; further west this time, past the Boulevard, where there was reckoned to be a bit more money about. Two years later, on opening the Anlaby Road (De la Pole Avenue) branch, the Board proudly announced that they had become property owners for the first time. Shortly afterwards the opening of a Tailoring Department at 7 Jarratt Street marked the Society's arrival in the city centre. This was followed, in 1899, by the acquisition of a large block of property at the corner of Jarratt Street and Charles Street to house the Drapery and Boot Departments; at the same time a Boot Repairing service was launched.

By the turn of the century, the Society's annual sales had reached £35,000 and more than 2,000 members were enjoying a dividend of 1/7¾d. on every pound they spent in its Stores. Expansion was now the order of the day.

CHAPTER THREE - YEARS OF RAPID EXPANSION 1901-1920

In the early days Co-operative advertising was often designed to appeal to the working man's sense of fairness and solidarity. Clothing, for example, was described as: 'All made in CWS factories under fair conditions of labour and no sweating!' 'Our Store is as moral as any in the country', another handbill assured members. And when buying footwear there was no question: 'Your DUTY and PRIVILEGE as a Trade Unionist, Friendly Society man and Co-operator is to buy only WHEATSHEAF BOOTS - made in our own factories. 2,729 hands employed under best conditions. These boots can be soled, soled and re-soled again.'

While the Society could scarcely justify lesser standards for its own workforce, a survey revealed that only about half of its 55 employees were in fact trade unionists. It was therefore laid down that all workers must be members of a trade union and, in future, hours and conditions would be jointly negotiated. This policy - though probably viewed as revolutionary at the time - seems to have made for orderly industrial relations, for throughout its existence the Hull Co-op suffered remarkably few labour disputes.

The Grocery Department was now forging ahead. By the close of 1902 it was trading from a chain of ten branch shops serving most of the city's then built up area. The Non-food departments, too, were benefiting from the coming of the electric tramway network, which had made it considerably easier for citizens to acquire the habit of shopping in the city centre.

Also in 1902 the Society opened its new General Offices on the corner of Jarratt Street and Kingston Square. For the first time, a qualified Secretary and Accountant - Mr. Henry Ferguson FCIS - was put in charge of the administration. But with dividends reaching record levels (two shillings in the pound on one never-to-be-repeated occasion), the crowds descending on Jarratt Street at divi-time soon necessitated an extension to the premises. Alternative arrangements therefore had to be made for the Educational activities previously held in the upstairs hall. So, with due ceremony, on 16th June 1904 a new Co-operative Institute was opened at 30 Albion Street by the Educational Chairman, Mr. Walter Litchfield.

Each year that Committee organised a Children's Gala on the Boulevard Football Ground, for which all young savers with the Society's Penny Bank received a free ticket. All the managers and staff rallied round to help on Gala Day and the crowds flocking to the field caused such havoc to the city's transport system that no one could fail to be aware of the Co-op. No other organisation was capable of staging such a huge attraction!

Mr. S. Marshall (in his book) personally noted the President, Mr. Arthur Boynton "in his usual dignified manner declaring the sports field open; J.M. James anxiously collecting the cash; the Society's Secretary helping in the bun department; W.H. Bailey assuming the role of compere; Walter Litchfield running about organising races; Jack Scarlett sweating at the ice cream stall; and Walter Horton providing music on his concertina". The only hitch was when the caterer misjudged 'the wants of the Co-operators in the eating line'. Profuse apologies had to be tendered to those who expected much but obtained little.

In 1904 the Society had 16 outlets listed in the very first edition of Hull's unique Corporation telephone directory. Not long afterwards, negotiations were in hand for a prominent site in the newly-constructed Jameson Street, where the Committee had visions of erecting 'a large central emporium'. The first instalment of this prestigious development opened for business on 29th August 1908.

Members' grocery orders were now being called for and delivered in all parts of Hull, Hessle, Anlaby, Anlaby Common, Kirkella, Westella, Cottingham, Sutton, Stoneferry, Hedon and Preston. But the advancement of the People's

Franklin Street branch. On the first floor was a Tea Room.

Typical early Co-operative propaganda, taken from a local Friendly Society Year Book.

Business drew ever fiercer criticism from its opponents. More letters appeared in the Press and one competitor even tried staging public debates. Fortunately, this was the kind of challenge that Messrs. James and Litchfield relished; the more the Society was vilified, the more vigorously, and ingeniously, they leapt to its defence.

From the start the Hull Co-op had been fortunate to have some versatile and well-known personalities on its Management Committee. Besides being passionate Co-operators, a number of them were councillors, aldermen, magistrates, chapel stewards and trade union officials, positions which brought them many valuable contacts. Often they were eminently practical people too, qualified in all kinds of building work, and thus ideally placed to nurture the Society's development. Councillor Tommy Hall, for example, was a trade union official but by trade a joiner; eventually he became a popular Lord Mayor of the city. Councillor Watson Boyes was a master builder; Mr. Jimmy Rice an engineer and union official; while Mr. Boynton was a foreman painter with the local authority.

With other daytime jobs to hold down, those involved were forced to attend to Co-operative business mainly in the evenings. The Board room was plainly no place for the feeble-bodied, for during one typical three-month period the President had to fulfil no fewer than 112 engagements! The other Committee members fared little better, with 86 each. These totals included 50 Board meetings, numerous Sub-Committees for Finance, Bakery & Grocery, Coal & Stables, and Drapery, and visits and functions of every kind.

Although the Society could now meet most of its members' everyday demands, facilities for stocking bulky articles like Furniture were still fairly limited. Anyone contemplating a major purchase was therefore encouraged to pay a visit to the CWS Showrooms in Manchester, where a wide choice of merchandise would always be available. By way of incentive, where the value of the sale exceeded £10, the Society undertook to refund the customer's excursion fare.

A Furniture removal service was also being promoted, with experienced packers: one man for 2/- an hour or two for half a crown. Whoever wrote the advert. had a wry sense of humour, for it read: 'Keep on moving! The oftener you move the more Divi you will get - if you use your own Society's vans.'

The Society had opened its first branch outside the city at Hessle (Gladstone Street) in 1905. A magic lantern and phonograph show was laid on to launch this tiny store, reportedly drawing quite a crowd. Cottingham (Exeter Street) opened the following year but this time the Co-operative Choral Society, under the baton of Mr. W.H. Carr, supplied the cultural dimension. The push into the East Riding continued in 1908, when the ailing Bridlington Co-op was absorbed, and throughout the ensuing decade, with outposts established at Howden (1911), South Cave (1914), Withernsea (1915), Newport (1918) and Hedon (1919).

Members were now pressing the Committee for a milk delivery service. After a rather protracted search, a suitable site for a Co-operative Dairy was found in Great Thornton Street, where Mr. Boynton performed the opening ceremony on 17th July 1915.

The outbreak of war against Germany in August 1914 threw up fresh challenges for those charged with running what was now a large and complex organisation. Practically the entire transport fleet was commandeered by the army, the drivers often volunteering to join up along with their vehicles. With staff numbers severely depleted, members had to be prevailed upon to carry home their purchases whenever possible. The sound of buzzer alarms, warning of Zeppelins approaching British shores under cover of darkness, frequently brought the

Branch No.11 - Dairycoates. By 1910 the Society's original rather cumbersome title had been shortened to the more practical version seen here.

One of the Society's smallest branches - Great Passage Street - in 1902.

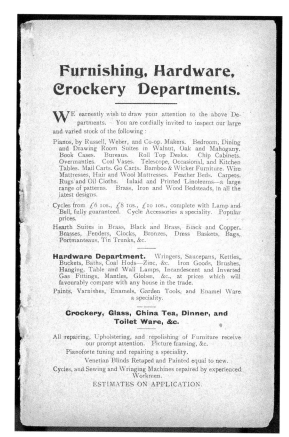

Furnishing, Hardware, Crockery Departments.

WE earnestly wish to draw your attention to the above Departments. You are cordially invited to inspect our large and varied stock of the following :

Pianos, by Russell, Weber, and Co-op. Makers. Bedroom, Dining and Drawing Room Suites in Walnut, Oak and Mahogany. Book Cases. Bureaus. Roll Top Desks. Chip Cabinets. Overmantles. Coal Vases. Telescope, Occasional, and Kitchen Tables. Mail Carts. Go Carts. Bamboo & Wicker Furniture. Wire Mattresses, Hair and Wool Mattresses. Feather Beds. Carpets. Rugs and Oil Cloths. Inlaid and Printed Linoleums—a large range of patterns. Brass, Iron and Wood Bedsteads, in all the latest designs.

Cycles from £6 10s., £8 10s., £10 10s., complete with Lamp and Bell, fully guaranteed. Cycle Accessories a speciality. Popular prices.

Hearth Suites in Brass, Black and Brass, Black and Copper. Brasses, Fenders, Clocks, Bronzes, Dress Baskets, Bags, Portmanteaus, Tin Trunks, &c.

Hardware Department. Wringers, Saucepans, Kettles, Buckets, Baths, Coal Hods—Zinc, &c. Iron Goods, Brushes, Hanging, Table and Wall Lamps, Incandescent and Inverted Gas Fittings, Mantles, Globes, &c., at prices which will favourably compare with any house in the trade.

Paints, Varnishes, Enamels, Garden Tools, and Enamel Ware a speciality.

Crockery, Glass, China Tea, Dinner, and Toilet Ware, &c.

All repairing, Upholstering, and repolishing of Furniture receive our prompt attention. Picture framing, &c.

Pianoforte tuning and repairing a speciality.

Venetian Blinds Retaped and Painted equal to new.

Cycles, and Sewing and Wringing Machines repaired by experienced Workmen.

ESTIMATES ON APPLICATION.

An extract from the quarterly Report to Members, July 1908.

Mr. Arthur John Boynton JP (President of the Society for a record 21 years - 1901-22). He also served as Chairman of Hull Rugby League F.C. There wasn't a prouder man on earth when the Airlie Birds won the Challenge Cup in 1914!

weekly Board meetings to an abrupt halt. But, though Hull was a prime target for enemy air raids, actual damage to Co-op property was minimal.

Despite the hostilities, some important business extensions went ahead, including a Slaughterhouse and Pork Butchery in Pelham Street, a Fruit Warehouse and Banana Ripening Depot in Pier Street and two farms, one at Wawne; the other at Weel near Beverley.

For thousands of families in the Hull area life was a constant battle against poverty. Making ends meet was a particular struggle whenever the wage-earner was out of work, fell ill or died. Before the advent of the Welfare State, the Co-op - like the trade unions and friendly societies - played a vital supporting role. The Hull Society, for example, regularly dispensed shopping vouchers from a special Distress Fund to members suffering hardship. And no effort was spared in canvassing the poorer districts of the city to explain to people how joining the Co-op might make a real difference to their lives. In 1918, following repeated agitation at Members' Meetings, it was also decided to add free life assurance to the portfolio of member benefits, to provide a small - but still helpful - 'cushion' for those left behind on the demise of a bread-winner.

The Minutes of the Wages Sub-Committee dated September 1919 make interesting reading, for they record the weekly pay scales about to be introduced for Co-op workers:

Junior Shop Assistants and Warehousemen:

Age	14	15	16	17	18	19	20
Male	16/-	18/-	21/-	24/-	35/-	40/-	45/-
Female	16/-	18/-	21/-	24/-	30/-	35/-	40/-

Adult Assistants:

	Age 21	22	23
Male	60/-	65/-	67/6d.
Female	44/-		

First Hands (to be appointed in all shops with 5 or more staff): 5/- above the scale rate.

Grocery Branch Managers: Commencing at £4 per week. Manageresses: 50/- Minimum.

Pork Branches: Males 67/6d. If house, light and fuel provided, wife to assist.
Females 50/-.   Assistants - as for Grocery.
General Grocery Manager: £7/10/-.
Shops Inspector: £4/15/-.
Head Warehouseman: 75/-.
Other Warehousemen (at age 21): 60/-

Motormen and Rulleymen:	60/-.	
Club Collectors:	Male	60/-
	Female	44/-.

Branch Drapery and Boots: Same rates as Grocery.
Coal Manager: £4/5/-.
Bakery Manager: £6.
Furnishing Manager: £5/10/-.
Works Manager: £5/10/-.

Clerks: Junior - Same rates as Shop Assistants.

	Senior - Age	21	22	23
	Male	60/-	65/-	72/6d.
	Female	44/-	47/-	

Sick pay and holidays with pay were also granted. Branch Managers, for example, were entitled to 12 working days a year and Pork Factory workers, a week. Note the obligation on butcher's wives to help out in the shop, in lieu of paying rent. Presumably this was an early example of 'creative accounting', where the branch made insufficient money to stand two wages. There was of course considerable prejudice against married women working in those days, as illustrated by this note which appeared in the *Hull Daily Mail* in November 1920:

Co-operative Society: We have received a letter alleging that a married woman with no children and husband in employment, is employed in one department. Our contributor should write to the Society

First phase of new Central Emporium, Jameson Street, 1908. The Store was extended in stages, reaching its full size in 1935 (Picture by courtesy of Ken Smith).

Commemorative mug produced by the CWS Longton Pottery and given to children attending the 1908 Gala Day. Some of this pottery has survived and turns up from time to time at 'bring and buy' sales.

itself, and get members to take up the question. We would point out that the Society is a free agent as an employer of labour.'

At the end of its third decade, the Society was operating from 43 Grocery branches spanning a wide arc from Flamboro' in the north to Howden in the west. Annual trade had surpassed the £1 million mark for the first time in 1919 and a membership of 32,000 was in sight. By any standards the Hull Co-operative Society had become very big business indeed.

Property on the coast at Withernsea, completed in 1915, typical of the many buildings designed for the Society by the Hull architect, Ald. T. Beecroft Atkinson: tall, sturdy, imposing and substantial. Most have retained their unmistakable Co-operative appearance long after passing to other owners.

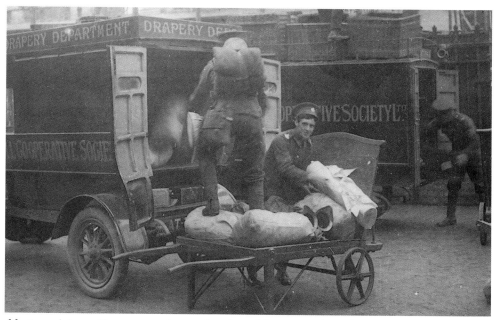

Mystery picture : Does anyone know what the soldiers were doing loading or unloading these Hull Co-op Drapery vans? Note the wicker hampers on top, which many years ago were used to transport household linens from factory to shop.

CHAPTER FOUR - DIFFICULT TIMES OVERCOME 1921-1939

The early 1920s turned out to be a testing time for the Society as the economic climate worsened. Unemployment was especially severe in the Hull area where, even in the better times, many workers had to make do with casual or seasonal jobs. The sensitivity of this situation was no doubt reflected in a Board ruling that 'if possible foreign goods are not to be bought for our shops'. With prices in the shops falling, to retain members' loyalty the Co-op was often forced to dispose of stocks below cost. The effect on its finances was serious.

Agriculture, too, was in a parlous state. In a single year (1922) the two farms alone lost £6,000, wiping out at a stroke half the Reserves which had taken 30 years to build up; consequently the dividend fell to 6d. in the £. To add to the troubles the popular President, Mr. Arthur Boynton, suddenly passed away in October 1922. Fortunately the baton of leadership quickly passed to a worthy successor, Councillor Watson Boyes.

The following year, with trading profits down yet again, it was decided to use the balance of the Reserves to prop up the 6d. dividend. Not in the habit of taking risks with the members' money, the Committee evidently felt that any further reduction - when families were experiencing such dire hardship - would harm the Society far more than carrying on with an empty kitty.

Optimistic that fortunes would soon improve, they pressed ahead with an ambitious building programme. It says much for their courage that, during those dark days, many finely appointed new branch shops were commissioned, while several existing ones were completely rebuilt. To make the best possible use of each site, flats, houses or halls were often incorporated into the plans.

As a gesture to help ease an acute local housing shortage, the Society had 18 semi-detached dwelling houses erected at Hessle. Built with the aid of a Government subsidy, they were offered to members either on rental or for sale at £600 each, the Co-op in the latter case being prepared to advance each purchaser up to £500 on mortgage. The development was aptly named Unity Avenue and most of the rented houses have since been bought by their sitting tenants.

Slowly but surely the tide turned from a sales and profits standpoint and before 1927 was out it became possible to step up the dividend, firstly to 9d. and then 1/- in the £. The Society also associated itself with the founding of Hull's University College, subscribing a useful £600 to its funds.

In February 1927 a tragic railway accident occurred close to Paragon Station, in which Mr. Wm. Gratrix, the Society's esteemed Secretary-Accountant, sustained serious injuries. Unable to resume full duties for over a year, he eventually had to retire on health grounds. The Committee invited Mr. Samuel Marshall, who had ably deputised in his absence, to take over as General Manager and Secretary, a position which he held with distinction for some 23 years.

One of Mr. Marshall's first tasks was to open negotiations with the Beverley Co-operative Society, whose members had put out feelers for an amalgamation. Unlike the Bridlington Co-op, this business was in a fairly healthy state and the merger was accomplished painlessly on 9th September 1929. On the same date Mr. Frederick Cant became Assistant Secretary and Mr. Harold Fenwick Head Office Cashier. A familiar figure in East Hull, Mr. Fenwick was for more than 40 years Master of the Salvation Army Band, in which a number of other Co-op employees also played.

With its earlier money worries behind it, the Society began to offer Pharmacy and Optical services and the launch of an employees' pension scheme was having the attention of the Board. For health reasons, Alderman Watson

Newbridge Road (Grocery Branch No.19) in 1922. In those days Grocery was clearly regarded as a man's world, the sole exception being the 'pastry girl' who ran the Confectionery section. Of course the Second World War changed all that!

After selling smoked fish for many years, the Society introduced boxed wet fish into Grocery branches in the 1920s. This postcard was designed to advertise the new service and promote an important local industry (By courtesy of Jean Oxley).

A vast extension to the Central Premises, featuring this long, winding arcade, was opened to the public in April 1923.

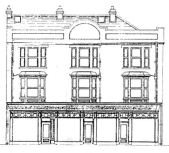

Mr. Atkinson's drawings for the Shaftesbury Avenue development (Branch no.47). As well as commodious Grocery and Butchery stores, he managed to fit three houses over the top plus another one at the rear.

Boyes had to give up the Presidency and Councillor Isaac Robinson took his place. A trusted friend of all Co-operators, Councillor Robinson went on to become a nationally-known figure in the Movement.

To provide better facilities for its Educational work, on 1st April 1931 the Society took over the former Trades & Labour Club in Kingston Square, for conversion into a Co-operative Institute. The Rt. Hon. A.V. Alexander, First Lord of the Admiralty and a prominent Co-operative Member of Parliament, came over to Hull to perform the opening ceremonies. Speeches in Kingston Square by Mr Alexander and Commander Kenworthy the local MP preceded a concert on the premises and a civic reception in the Guildhall. That evening, after an organ recital and the voice of 'wonderful boy soprano' Master Stainton, a Gigantic Mass Meeting took place in the City Hall. Supported by a cluster of civic dignitaries and Co-op worthies, the First Lord again addressed the gathering. Clearly, Co-operators didn't believe in doing things by half measure!

The Bakery suffered a serious outbreak of fire one night in October 1932, with the loss of much of the property and stock. Luckily there were no personal injuries but, when the police called at his home, it seems the man with the Bakery keys was out doing a spot of courting, with the keys in his pocket. Once he had seen his lady friend safely home, he dashed to the scene but by then the fire was well under control.

Remarkably, in an area plagued by chronic unemployment and low, irregular family incomes, the Society's growth rate regularly outpaced the national average during the 1930s. The Society put this paradox down to its well-oiled propaganda machine, run by its enthusiastic Publicity Manager, Mr. J.M. Peddie. As a experiment Mr. Peddie had put together a team of four keen young Grocery Assistants - Ernie Teall, Harold Foster, Eddie

Langfield and Doug Widdowson - to canvass the new housing estates that were springing up all over the city. Doug Widdowson revealed their tactics: 'We used to watch for people moving in and then descend on them before the opposition got there. We would reel off as many Co-operative services as we could think of and then try to persuade them to part with a shilling to join. With free delivery, credit and dividend on offer, most housewives just couldn't resist! Mr. Marshall was so pleased with our results that he rewarded us with promotion to First Hands.' Two permanent canvassers were later set on to comb systematically through the records and chase up lapsed members on the doorstep. At one time the Publicity Section even deployed a loudspeaker van to bring the Co-operative message home to Hull's sprawling suburbia.

The year 1935 was a particularly momentous one. It was the year when the Employees' Superannuation Fund paid out its first pensions. To give the 27 retirees a fitting send off, a Concert-Meeting was staged for all the staff. Jack Prince, local editor of *The Wheatsheaf* magazine, was there to record the memorable event: 'As each recipient came forward to receive his gift and diploma from the Lord Mayor, Mr. Marshall had the packed City Hall rocking in laughter with witty anecdotes about his or her service.' Thanks to the 'Super. Fund' male and female Co-op workers, when they reached the age of 65 and 60 respectively, could now retire in relative comfort. Soon afterwards the Society enrolled its 50,000th member. The City Hall was the venue for yet another celebration - a Staff Dance and Monstre (*sic*) Whist Drive.

The business had now entered its most prolific phase of expansion. Branches at Greenwood Avenue, Gillshill Road, Willerby Square, Anlaby Common, Hessle High Road, North Ferriby, First Avenue, Wold Road, Northfield (Hessle) and County Road South were all added to the Co-operative map during the 1930s. So

Horse drawn float setting off from Hessle Northgate branch to join the International Co-operators' Day parade in 1926. The rulleyman, Jack Cobb, was a well-known figure in Hessle (Picture by courtesy of Mr. P. Howlett).

Taxing the Workers' Savings : When the National Government imposed extra taxation on Co-operatives in 1933, Hull Co-op members delivered a 62,000 signature petition to Westminster - a nationwide record! The powers-that-be took no notice, but it wasn't all bad news : thanks to all the free publicity, the Society enrolled 5,000 new members in just six months.

Toll Gavel, Beverley Drapery Branch, 1933. At the door are George Frost (who later became a talented Display Manager with the Society), Joyce Lewis and Annie Galbraith (Picture by courtesy of Mrs J. Eaton).

One of the country branches - Wallingfen (Newport) before and after its 1935 rebuild. In the later view there is a good display of clothing etc. for a village shop. The villagers of Newport had two Co-ops to choose from, both managing to trade almost side by side for nearly 50 years.

popular had Co-op shopping become that many of the older branches were now bursting at their seams and had to be either extended or relocated to roomier premises.

The purpose-built shops were all fitted out to a high standard, the main building contract usually being entrusted to the Society's own Works Department, while specialist trades were contracted out to various experts. The contracts let in respect of First Avenue branch in 1936 illustrate this practice:
Steelwork - Messrs. King & Co. - £232/-/-
Tiling - Messrs. Dawber, Townsley - £155/16/-
Precast floor beams - Rapid Precast Floors Ltd. - £171/-/-
Precast stonework - Hull Concrete Stone Co. Ltd. - £26/8/-
Sunblinds - Messrs. Hy. Jordan & Son - £9/10/-
Shop fronts - Godolphin Metal Fronts Ltd. - £118/-/-
Plumbing - Messrs. Drape and Upton - £122/-/-
Asphalting - Northern Asphalt & Roofing Works Co. - £18/2/9d.
Flour bins and chutes - Leeds Co-op Society Ltd. - £34/15/-

Yet, despite enjoying overwhelming public support, the Society was still encountering the fiercest hostility to its development plans. In one instance, vested interests conspired to thwart all attempts to buy land in the Bricknell Avenue area. Such tactics only made Management more determined and, by devious means and much to the annoyance of certain prominent anti-Co-operators, they eventually managed to acquire an undeniable title to a large corner site. After several abortive attempts, plans for Grocery and Butchery stores and three other shops were finally passed by the local authority. However, when the premises were half built, the Society was served with an injunction to cease work pending a decision in the High Court. Interested parties were now alleging that building permission had been wrongly given.

The Hull Corporation joined forces to resist the charges and Learned Counsel had to be consulted (Mr. Marshall even went to London for a top-level meeting with Sir Stafford Cripps) before the Society finally emerged victorious, winning its case with costs. Shortly after the premises opened, torrential rain flooded the surrounding district to a depth of about a foot and the indefatigable Co-operators had to walk-the-plank to get in and out of the shop! The surplus shops were sold off, the project proving highly profitable, as did a similar venture at Willerby Square.

Just as the Society acted as agents for the Co-operative Insurance Society until it built up sufficient business to warrant opening a local office, so similar facilities were granted to the Co-operative Permanent Building Society; all Co-operators saving to buy a home were urged to take out membership. Early in 1936 the Society entered Funeral Furnishing and this important department soon developed into one of the leading undertakers in East Yorkshire. The growing popularity of home and foreign travel provided another avenue of expansion, with agencies for both the CWS Travel Service and the Workers' Travel Association being set up within the Central Premises.

'Made in your own factories . . by your own workers . . with your own capital . . demand CWS always!' So ran a poster often seen in Co-op shop windows at this time. A steadfast supporter of the Co-operative Wholesale Society, the Hull Co-op constantly urged its members to choose CWS productions when shopping. Besides representing excellent quality, these products earned the retail society a dividend, which all helped to boost its own members' divi. Wheatsheaf (canned goods), Crumpsall (cream crackers), Waveney (potato crisps), JP (sauce), Lutona (cocoa), MP (puddings), Sutox (suet), Shortex (cooking fat), Pulvo (cleaner) and Pelaw (boot polish) are just a few of the familiar CWS names that regularly rolled off the tongue of the most devout Co-op shoppers. Then there was Excelda - widely acclaimed as the finest flour for baking - and 99 Tea, still a celebrated Co-op brand today. By 1937 the Hull Society was buying 96% of all its groceries through the 'Wholesale', one of the best loyalty records in the Movement. It was a similar story in Non-foods, with over four-fifths of all footwear, drapery and furniture sourced through the CWS.

Co-operatives have always been internationally-minded and so it was no surprise to find a paragraph in the Hull Society's December 1937 Report, appealing to members to 'extend the hand of friendship to their brothers and sisters' in war-torn Spain, which was in the throes of civil war. Special sixpenny coupons were on sale in all stores as part of a concerted effort by the British Co-operative Movement to provide food and milk for women and children in the stricken territories.

In the spring of 1939, Co-operators from all over Britain converged on Hull when the Society hosted the Annual Congress of the Co-operative Women's Guild. Some cine-film footage of this event was recently discovered and has been preserved for posterity in the National Co-operative Film Archive.

As the 'thirties drew to a close, trading conditions in East Yorkshire became more and more depressed. One international crisis after another had unsettled the public mood, making people extra cautious about parting with their cash. Food prices were falling yet again and even more of the region's bread-winners found themselves thrown out of work. But, thanks to a decade of prudent investment and sound progress, the Hull Co-op was in a better shape than ever to face the trials and tribulations that lay ahead.

The Co-op stand at the Civic and Trades Exhibition, City Hall in 1936. No one could possibly be left in any doubt about the wide range of services the Society had to offer.

A typical 1930s-style shop front : Queensgate, Bridlington Grocery and Butchery. During the war Army and Air Force personnel training on the park opposite developed a hearty appetite for the Confectionery sections buns, which sold for 6d. a dozen!

In readiness for food rationing every citizen had to register with a trader of their choice. So many families signed up with the Co-op that an 'army' of clerks and typists had to be recruited to Jarratt Street simply to cope with all the extra paperwork.

CHAPTER 5 - 'BOMBED, BLITZED AND BUNKERED, BUT NEVER BEATEN' 1939-45

From the perspective of our relatively settled times it is far from easy to appreciate how extensively an international war disrupted business routine. Here are just a few of the ways in which the wits and energies of the Society's Management were put to the test during those turbulent years:

- The evacuation of families to other districts and closure of city schools sharply reduced the demand for food and milk,
- Precious food stocks had to be dispersed around the rural branches in case the Central Warehouse received an enemy 'hit',
- A mass training programme had to be organised to acquaint all staff with First Aid, Anti-Gas and fire fighting techniques,
- Nightly for five years the Office records and valuables had to be ferried out into the countryside for safe keeping,
- The selling prices laid down by law often left insufficient margin to cover working expenses and normal dividend rates,
- Compulsory insurance for stocks and property added an extra £10,000 a year to expenses (but, as it happens, was soon to prove its worth),
- In vital trades like Baking, pacts had to be entered into with competing firms to ensure continuity of public supplies,
- To comply with one rather bizarre Government Order, the word 'Hull' had to be painted out of the Society's name on all shop fascias, a measure intended to confound the enemy, should they dare to set foot on East Yorkshire soil!

As in the previous war, the Society lost dozens of its experienced employees to military service. Their work was given to temporary 'dilutees', many of whom were quite unused to the little peculiarities of Co-operative practice. With the menfolk away, women entered shopwork in a big way. Some, rapidly and quite unexpectedly, found themselves promoted to dizzy heights of responsibility - such as First Assistant in a Grocery branch - that had traditionally been regarded as male preserves.

The authorities took over the Society's Slaughterhouse and commandeered a number of its motor lorries. Fortunately, while war clouds were gathering, Management had acted promptly to order a fleet of electric vehicles for local deliveries. With their limited range they were less likely to be useful to the Army and were of course unaffected by petrol rationing.

Every branch had to be fitted with 'black out' door traps and some means of shelter for the staff. At Jameson Street two air raid shelters were provided in the basement (one for males; the other for females), while the First Aid area was equipped with an emergency generator intended to be powered by members of staff pedalling a tandem cycle. A comical idea, perhaps, when seen from this distance in time, but in 1940 deadly serious.

With so many factories diverted to military needs, it became increasingly difficult to obtain sufficient rations for all the Co-op's members. As sources of supply and wholesale prices were all under strict ministerial control, the Society's buyers were unable to exercise choice and denied the usual benefits of bulk buying. Sometimes this had unusual consequences. As mentioned earlier, the Hull Co-op had always done a big trade in lines manufactured by the Co-operative Wholesale Society. Now it had no choice but to sell other brands and likewise private traders were often forced to take CWS. When things returned to normal, the demand for CWS products increased noticeably. After trying them for the first time, customers of rival shops had evidently acquired a liking for them and gone back insisting upon CWS and no other!

From February 1941 all business premises had to be constantly fire-watched and tribute must be paid to the employees who volunteered for this duty; on more than one occasion they managed to save the Society's valuable possessions from annihilation.

'Abundance in Wartime' was the title given to this shot of the Arcade Grocery window which the Society forwarded to the Ministry of Information for use in official propaganda. The idea was prompted by Lord Haw Haw, whose mischievous 'Jarmany calling!' broadcasts claimed the British people were on the point of starving. The display was created by Mr. Sidney Rodmell, who won many awards for window dressing (Picture by courtesy of Mrs S. Walker).

New Cleveland Street (Branch No.16) sporting a wartime frontage, with the word Hull painted out by Government order. Note also the peep-hole windows which helped maintain black-out and avoided having to replace expensive plate-glass. Because of rationing they would be set out with dummy products.

Motor ambulance donated to the city to commemorate the Society's Golden Jubilee Year - 1940. With the civilian services working under tremendous pressure, this practical gesture proved immensely valuable.

Before : Central Emporium, Jameson Street, Hull. During the 1930s it was undoubtedly one of the finest Co-operative Stores in the country.

After : The same Store in ruins in May 1941. Fortunately no staff were injured and none lost a single day's pay as a result.

Hull in fact turned out to be one of Britain's most heavily blitzed cities. In nearly 100 air raids more than 86,000 homes were damaged or demolished; about 1,200 citizens were killed and 3,000 sustained injuries; 152,000 found themselves temporarily homeless. Nearly all the Society's Branches and Departments were damaged in the raids, its premises being hit by bomb or blast more than 200 times. Brindley Street Grocery was the first shop affected, on 26th June 1940, and Holland Street - on 17th March 1945 - the last. Two branches, Hedon Road and Sculcoates Lane, were wiped out completely. Holland Street Drapery was bombed out a second time only days after reopening further along the road and business was promptly moved back to its original site. And the ruins of Franklin Street branch were seen by Winston Churchill when he came to Hull at the height of the war to inspect the devastation for himself. Shop fronts were frequently blown out but the Works Department soon seemed to have them boarded up and made fit for 'business as usual'.

The worst blow came during the night of 7/8th May 1941 when the Society's pride and joy, its recently-modernised Central Store in Jameson Street, was set on fire from end to end. Practically all the city centre stores were hit at once and, owing to the demands on the Fire Service, the raging inferno was simply left to burn itself out, destroying virtually the whole of the premises together with £97,000 worth of stocks.

During the same attack the Jarratt Street Offices were showered with incendiary bombs; only the valiant efforts of the fire-watching team prevented their total loss. According to an eye-witness it was the General Manager, Mr. Marshall, who personally manned the fire-pump that kept the flames in check. At the time thousands of bank notes were in the safes ready for dividend payment the next day. Miraculously they were saved and, though water was cascading down the stairs and debris

was scattered everywhere, business was only suspended for half a day. Had there been a different twist of fate, no official compensation would have been forthcoming and the people of Hull would have missed out on half a year's divi. The same evening a land mine wiped out the Main Street Garage; 11 petrol vehicles and a dozen horse-rulleys were lost or severely damaged.

The tide of devastation returned the following night. Osborne Street Grocery Warehouse went up in flames, with the loss of £17,063 worth of valuable food and tobacco stocks. Hessle Road Pork Butchery and the Cattle Lairage in Commerce Lane were also demolished.

Nearly all Co-operative propaganda work was suspended for the duration but the Guilds carried on undaunted, their weekly meetings affording a peaceful refuge to those grappling with the privations of life on the Home Front. Sit and Sew, Dressmaking and Make and Mend appeared on the syllabus and members made up parcels of 'comforts' for those far away. To keep them in touch with happenings at home, free copies of *Reynolds News* and *The Wheatsheaf* were despatched to every Co-op member and employee known to be serving abroad.

As their contribution to the war effort the Educational Committee laid on free entertainment in the Institute for any soldiers, sailors and airmen billeted in the area. 'Members of the British, Canadian, American and West Indian Forces gather three nights a week for this very *clean* form of entertainment,' the Committee were at pains to point out. With attendances averaging 700 a week, House Full signs were often needed.

In 1941 there was a change in the Presidential Chair, Mr. Aubrey Peel (the President since 1936) being succeeded by Mr. Walter Kirk. Mr. Kirk was a great ambassador for the local Co-operative Movement; for many years he served as Chairman of the Hull Printers Ltd.,

Hedon Road Branch - a total loss on 16th April 1941. With every scrap of food vitally important the staff sifted through the wreckage and managed to salvage 90% of the stock (Picture by courtesy of the City Record Office).

Temporary premises acquired for the Furnishing Department, at the corner of Beverley Road and Fountain Road.

Cast list for 'The Pageant of the People'. Can you find a name you know?

The Speaking Cast
++++

Speaker : W. A. Prickett.

Prologue ...	S. Goodier,	Woman ...	Margaret Kitching
2nd Man ...	J. Lester,	Young Woman	Elsie M. Denman,
3rd Man ...	K. Dick,	Magistrate ...	C. Metham,
Captain ...	H. Mays,	Owen ...	F. Jackson,
Lieutenant ...	F. Woollons,	1st Child ...	B. Blades,
Washington ...	W. Everett,	2nd Child ...	B. Thomas,
George III ...	F. Parker,	3rd Child ...	J. Ellis,
Weaver ...	W. Capes,	4th Child ...	S. Newall,
His Wife ...	A. Taylor,	Politician ...	F. Woollons,
Little Girl ...	Joyce M. Burrell,	Scotch Artisan	T. Ramsay,
Boy	David Cox,	Smithies ...	C. Needler,
Overseers V. Newdick, F. Billany,		Cooper ...	T. Fenby,
D. Cantrell, C. Needler,		Daly ...	A. Linton,
Owner ...	E. Strodder,	Standring ...	E. Cowton,
Citizen ...	A. Linton,	Howarth ...	W. F. Hodson,
Desmoulins ...	N. Parker,	Bent ...	W. Judd,
John Bright ...	A. Randerson,	Mrs. Dunlop	Lucie L. Glasby,
Hill	H. Mays,	1st Man ...	K. Dick,
Son	Brian Kirby,	Housemaid	Doris Capes,
Leach	D. Robson,	Woman ...	Elsie M. Denman,
Mary ...	Doris Timson,	Tweedale ...	W. Capes,
Cooper ...	T. Fenby,	George ...	C. Metham,
Sam	J. Lester,	Dr. Dunlop	S. Goodier,
Woman ...	M. Fall,	Holyoake ...	I. Robinson,
Boys ...	F. Billany, E. Pickering,	Old Women ...	C. A. Cocksworth,
Charwomen R. Boothby, E. Booth,			F. Levitt,
Colonists : B. Bell, E. Cooper,		Miles Ashworth	W. Everett,
Orator ...	S. Goodier,	Bugler ...	C. Richardson,
Leader ...	G. de Boer,		

Soldiers : C.S.M.—V. C. Brown. Privates—W. Chapman, W. Hopper, M. Oates, G. Scott, J. Stamforth, B. Westerby, and Tpr. J. Newman.

Little Man : Alfred Harriman.

CORPS DE BALLET

Joan Atkinson,	Ivy Hammond,	Jean O'Pray,
Irene Birtles,	Sylvia Hickey,	Kathleen O'Pray,
Pat Bradley,	Betty Holden,	Beryl Rich,
Cynthia Cruickshank,	Ruby Lindsay,	Kathleen Bradley,
Jessie Drury,	Nancy Lyell,	Eileen Rands,
Gladys Guymer,	Eileen Moore,	Joan Turner.

[5]

also as Secretary to the Hull Co-operative People's Bank. Always immaculately dressed - in black jacket, white stiff-collared shirt and striped trousers, his habit of sporting a white carnation in his buttonhole was especially well-known in the city.

Local efforts to mark the centenary of the Rochdale Pioneers uplifted war-weary spirits in 1944. The BBC Dramatist L. Du Garde Peach (grandly-styled Chief Pageant Master) had written a pageant especially for the occasion, to be performed in theatres up and down the land, chiefly by amateur casts. *The Pageant of the People* opened at Hull's New Theatre for a whole week on 31st July. In charge of the proceedings was the noted London producer, Claud Jenkins, assisted by Hull's own Madame Sharrah, while Edgar Sales ably officiated as Chorus Master. Some 200 amateur artistes, supported by countless backstage helpers, took part in this notable production, which not only enthralled its capacity audiences but also gave hours of much-needed fun to everyone involved.

In February 1945 a member of the Hull Society's Management Committee, Mr. J.M. Peddie MBE, was voted on to the Board of the Co-operative Wholesale Society. It was the first time that a Hull nominee had been successful and Mr. Peddie rendered outstanding service in this capacity for some 20 years, going on to become a Director and Vice Chairman of the Co-operative Insurance Society, a Director of the Co-operative Permanent Building Society and, from 1957 to 1965, National Chairman of the Co-operative Political Party.

When peace finally came in 1945, there were still some 600 male and 435 female employees away in the Forces. The Society eased their gradual rehabilitation back into Civvy Street, when it came, in two important ways. Firstly, by promising to keep their jobs open. Secondly, through a special Welcome Home Fund which provided each returning service-person with a £5 gift voucher and tickets for a series of Victory Dances at the Madeley Street Baths. Sadly, forty employees never returned; their names were recorded in the Half-Yearly Report of March 1946 beneath a fitting tribute to those 'who paid the supreme sacrifice in the campaign for peace and freedom'.

Considering Hull was in the front line, it was remarkable that not one employee had been killed or injured while on Society duty during the entire six years of war. Moreover, thanks to the skills of Management and the readiness of staff at all times to restore order out of chaos, the Co-op's huge food and fuel distribution business had been maintained without a single day's interruption. It was a magnificent achievement - and one for which thousands of East Yorkshire families had every reason to be grateful. Hence the title of this chapter, which has been taken from a pamphlet which the General Manager prepared in 1945 to show just how the Society weathered the storms of those fateful years.

Three Hull Co-op personalities at a Conference in 1951 : Jim Peddie (Vice President); Samuel Marshall (General Manager and Secretary) and Walter Kirk (President). Note the carnation in Mr.Kirk's lapel, for which he was renowned.

A Co-op shop in all but name : Hargreaves Grocery, Endike Lane. With new building licences scarcer than gold, the Society had to resort to buying up private businesses to ease the pressure on existing branches. Known as the 'pantry shops' they continued trading under their old names for several years, to meet the complexities of the rationing scheme.

CHAPTER SIX - A TIME TO REBUILD AND MODERNISE 1945-63

The Society emerged from the war battered and bruised but financially very sound. An upbeat note in the Balance Sheet boasted that its outside investments, which now exceeded £2 millions, would have been sufficient to repay members the whole of their share capital, leave a surplus of £174,000 and still provide enough working capital to carry on business as normal.

A major preoccupation for the next few years was what to do about the Central Premises. With the city centre lying in ruins, all the leading store operators were anxious to re-establish a full trading presence without delay. The Hull Corporation, however, had taken the opportunity presented by the devastation to engage town planning experts to advise on the future layout and design of the city.

Sir Patrick Abercrombie's radical *Plan for Kingston upon Hull*, published in 1944, envisaged closing Jameson Street altogether and relocating the central shopping core en bloc to the Osborne Street area. This would have entailed setting up a Co-op Department Store on a fresh site and the Management Committee, while not wanting to appear obstructionists, feared this might prejudice the Society's War Damage Compensation claims. No fewer than 53 other Co-op properties were also scheduled to be affected by town planning proposals over the next 25 years. Negotiations over reparations dragged on endlessly and the Society joined forces with those in two other blitzed cities - Plymouth and Birmingham - to press their case before a special Parliamentary Committee.

Meanwhile, the 'tug of war' between the Corporation and the traders over the latter's freehold rights, and the location of the shops, resulted in yet more planning experts' reports and public inquiries. This only compounded the delay and people were deserting Hull in droves to shop in other towns. Permission was therefore pressed for to erect a temporary one-storey shop on the Co-op's Jameson Street site, which opened in time for Christmas 1947. An extension, to provide a 'shop window' for the Furnishing stocks held at Fountain Road, followed in 1950.

Early 1948 saw food prices tumble as the Co-op responded to the Labour Government's call to help ease the cost of living. Butter, bacon and cheese came down by 2d. a lb., preserves and margarine by 1d. a lb. and bread by ½d. for a large loaf. The move was intended to give a lead to other shopkeepers, but in practice few followed suit. Moreover, the total benefit to each household turned out to be rather meagre, for the slimmer profit margins on these staple items simply shaved 2d. in the £ off the dividend! After a year the experiment was quietly dropped.

Modernisation was now the watchword in all Departments. The Dairy and the Bakery were completely re-equipped with 'state of the art' machinery, while the Traffic Department bade a sad farewell to its ever-faithful rulley-horses. The 73 Grocery stores gradually benefited from refrigeration, hot water supplies, tobacco safes and new shop fronts. At one stage the Society also contemplated developing a Co-operative Village, at the corner of Leads Road and Sutton Road, in which to centralise all its food factories, warehouses and transport depots, together with housing for the workforce. Extensive talks were held with the site owners but drainage problems eventually put paid to this futuristic project.

After years of frustration it was finally established in 1950 that the Central Premises could be rebuilt broadly on their former site. Plans were immediately drawn up in the CWS Architects' Office for a store much larger than the pre-war version. Many more years were to elapse, however, before negotiations with the War Damage Commission were finally concluded and all the Society's claims satisfactorily met.

Sales topped £5 million a year for the first time

The temporary premises in Jameson Street (often referred to as the Prefab.). Today's shopkeepers please note : A chair was provided for customers at each serving point, a sign that shopping was perhaps a more leisurely experience in those days. This was also one of the first buildings in Hull to be illuminated with fluorescent tubes.

in 1952. With more than 2,000 workers the Hull Co-op was easily one of East Yorkshire's biggest employers. However, while membership was still rising, share capital was now in decline as members drew on their savings to buy and furnish their homes and invest in those comforts that the war economy had denied them. There was a heavy demand for electric washing machines, cleaners and 'fridges as families set about updating their domestic routines. The coming of television to the North of England in 1951, followed by the Coronation, created an enormous interest in TV sets and the Co-op rapidly emerged as one of the region's leading dealers.

The falling share capital posed no real problem, for the Society had far more capital than it could profitably use in trade. One of the people responsible for this happy situation was the General Manager and Secretary, Mr. Samuel Marshall JP FCIS FLAA, who retired from office on 10th September 1952. 'S.M.' could look back on a career spanning 47 years during which his employer had grown from a tiny business into a multi-million pound concern with 73 Grocery, 54 Butchery and 6 Non-food shops and major Dairy, Bakery, Funeral, Coal, Drug and Optical interests.

Mr. Marshall's superb business acumen, intolerance of waste and love of fair play earned him such universal respect that he is still fondly remembered today. His whole life was characterised by the utmost integrity and devotion to Co-operative principles. Inevitably there were those who tried to argue that his management style was over-cautious. Such critics were swiftly rebuffed with a reminder that he was 'a custodian of the People's savings'. Without a degree of caution 'our Society would not have been in the happy position it enjoys today, for it would probably have two or three white elephants, whereas it exits 1951 like a Lion', he asserted in his final Christmas message to the staff. It was tragic that someone who had done so much to put the Employees'

Superannuation Fund on a sound footing did not live to enjoy its fruits. Just three months after laying down the burdens of office, Mr. Marshall suddenly passed away.

The top post was now split in two. Mr. Arnold Barnes from the Woodhouse Society became General Manager, while the Secretaryship passed to Mr. Fred Cant until his own retiral three years later. Mr. Cant had worked alongside Mr. Marshall and served on the staff of the Beverley and Hull Societies since 1914.

A new era began in the Grocery Department on 22nd February 1954 when Greenwood Avenue became the first branch to convert to self-service, followed a week later by 440 Anlaby Road.

Following approval of the plans, test piling began at Jameson Street towards the end of 1954. Building was originally scheduled to take place in stages over three years to avoid undue disruption to trade, but the timescale soon proved wildly optimistic as the project encountered one obstacle after another. At one stage an Act of Parliament had to be pushed through to obtain the necessary consent to build over a short stretch of the Queen's Highway at the rear; this delayed progress by some two years. Eleven years eventually went by before the Society's impressive new headquarters were ready for their official opening.

Towards the close of 1956 members of the Pocklington & District Co-operative Society voted to merge with Hull. The assets included four rural branch shops together with Grocery, Butchery, Non-food and Coal operations in the market town itself. Combined membership now stood at 71,200, with around 100 new members still joining every week. With 96% of members' capital profitably re-invested, the Society's finances had never been stronger. Yet signs were starting to emerge that all was not entirely well. A definite slowing down in the tempo of Grocery sales was detected. The trend was by no

By 1961 the Hull Co-op had 19 mobile Grocery shops on the road. Powered by re-chargeable electric batteries and staffed by a driver and assistant, they were a boon on the city's new housing estates, where permanent shopping facilities were non-existent (Picture by courtesy of Innes Studios).

'Good morning madam, please take a basket'. Customers found self-service bewildering at first, but gradually they appreciated the speedier service and wider choice. For the Society it increased sales and reduced personnel costs.

46

means peculiar to East Yorkshire; all over Britain Co-ops were finding trade harder to win as competition intensified. After being the first large-scale retailers, they were now paying the price as their rivals made up for lost time.

A particular threat was the discount store. Often housed in a cheaply-converted warehouse or old cinema, it exploited the 'cash and carry' principle to the full to drive down costs and prices. Pressure from these cut-price merchants soon killed off Resale Price Maintenance in the food trade, a comfortable arrangement that for years had kept the selling prices of branded goods identical in all kinds of shop. Co-op practice had always been to sell at these prices and return any surplus made as dividend. But in 1959 the Hull Society was forced to adopt its own Cut Price Policy, a move that was bound to put the squeeze on the all-important dividend rate, linked as this was to the average profit margin. Shoppers found it hard to accept that they couldn't have both high dividends and discount prices; feeling let down, many simply voted with their feet and took their custom elsewhere.

The realisation that, after years of unchallenged growth, the Co-ops were running out of steam had prompted the setting up of an Independent Commission in 1955, chaired by Hugh Gaitskell MP, Deputy Leader of the Labour Party. Its brief was to enquire into the state of the entire Co-operative Movement and come up with recommendations for its future. It so happened that in 1958 Hull's Jim Peddie had been chosen as President of the annual Co-operative Congress - the highest honour the Movement can bestow on one of its members. That autumn it fell to him to preside over a second Congress called specially to debate the Commission's far reaching and controversial findings.

The Hull Co-op had its share of colourful characters but none better known than James Peddie MBE. He had first found fame as a child by writing a Christmas carol for his church and winning an essay competition organised by the Savings Bank. Then, aged 19, at Hull Technical College, he became Britain's youngest economics lecturer. After a spell at the London School of Economics, Mr. Marshall recruited him as the Hull Co-op's Publicity Manager, a role in which he displayed singular flair and imagination.

But it was his top-level involvement in the CWS and Co-op Party that eventually brought him into contact - and later friendship - with most of the senior Labour politicians of the day. In 1961 he was elevated to the peerage as Baron Peddie of Kingston upon Hull and became an active member of the House of Lords. The Hull Co-op gave a Guildhall Dinner in his honour.

A man of deep Co-operative and Socialist convictions, Peddie was a pugnacious fighter for the causes he held dear. He was a powerful orator too, who loved sweeping an audience to its feet with the sheer force of his argument. His practical view of life was spiced with a dry, dead-pan sense of humour - the hallmark of a true Yorkshireman. But, despite achieving national eminence, he never forgot his Hull roots and was content to remain just 'Jim' to all who knew him.

The year 1961 saw two momentous changes on the administration side: Firstly, Walter Kirk stepped down after 20 years in the Presidential chair. He was succeeded by Bakery Manager Frank Johnson, whose own service was cut short by his untimely death two years later, after which the leadership passed to Ronald Gray. And in November the General Office moved from its old home at 26 Jarratt Street to the third floor of the new Jameson Street Store, just in time for the Christmas dividend pay-out.

By 1962 the Hull Society had one of the largest trading areas of any in Britain. To reflect its growing influence outside the city, a Members' Meeting resolved to re-name it the HULL AND EAST RIDING CO-OPERATIVE SOCIETY

Gillshill Road Grocery and Butchery, as extended and converted to self-service in 1955. Note the hoist on the side wall for lifting bulky goods into the upstairs stock rooms, a standard feature of most Hull Co-op Grocery shops (Picture by courtesy of Innes Studios).

HULL CO-OPERATIVE SOCIETY LIMITED
MARKET STREET, POCKLINGTON
SELF SERVICE STORE

Open for Business - Monday December 1st

What is Self Service?

Self Service is the most modern method of shopping by Self Selection, and it has proved to be the most acceptable method of shopping for the busy housewife

How do I do my Shopping?

In a Self Service Shop there is an entrance and an exit. On entering, the customer finds a stand with baskets, takes one, and then enters the store proper

The customer then helps herself to the goods displayed in the Self Service fittings and places them in the basket provided, making her selections as leisurely or quickly as she wishes

All goods are clearly marked so you DO KNOW what you pay for every item

The layout of the store is designed to allow easy shopping and our sales staff will always be pleased to help and advise customers. Provisions (Bacon, Butter, Cheese, Sausages, etc.) will be displayed in and sold from a modern refrigerated display unit

When you have completed your shopping, you go to the check-out counter, where your purchases are added by an assistant on a modern electric calculator. On payment, you receive an itemised totalled list together with your dividend check

The basket is returned to the stand and your shopping completed with a considerable saving of time

Cigarettes, Tobacco, Bread and Confectionery, Sweets and Chocolates, Ice Cream and Frozen Foods are obtainable without having to enter the Self Service Section

Our Grocery Manager—Mr. E. W. Ainsley, together with his experienced staff are at your service

You have needed better shopping facilities. We are proud to offer you the best that modern science and engineering has produced

"OUR SPECIAL OPENING OFFER"

The first 100 customers spending £1 or more in cash will

receive FREE one fine quality food parcel - value 4/6

SELF SERVICE IS QUICK SERVICE   DIVIDEND TOO OF COURSE !

SELF SERVICE IS QUICK SERVICE — DIVIDEND TOO OF COURSE !

THIS ILLUSTRATION SHOWS THE INTERIOR LAYOUT OF OUR NEW FOOD STORE

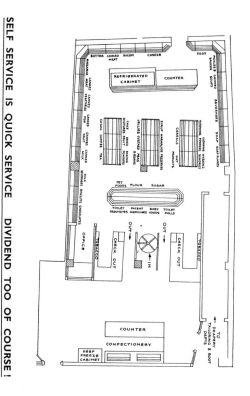

48

LTD. This trend was reinforced in 1963 when the 2,300-member Market Weighton and District Co-operative Society voted for a merger. Five shops with annual sales of £250,000 were transferred in on 7th September and total membership then peaked at 81,122.

Thanks to widening car ownership, few parts of East Yorkshire now lay beyond the catchment area of a Co-op store; opportunities to open more branches were thus few and far between. But one unusual new venture was a summer-only Camp Shop on the Municipal Caravan Park at Withernsea, catering for the holidaymaker's every need. Its opening on 31st May 1963 momentarily brought the total number of Grocery stores to 90.

The very next day saw the tally dip to 89 again, as the Board embarked on a Rationalisation Plan designed to tackle two pressing problems: population drift and duplication. As the Hull Corporation's slum clearance programme moved into top gear, the trade of many older Co-op shops was fading away as families were rehoused en masse from the overcrowded

Victorian streets of the inner-city to vast new estates on the outskirts, all attractively laid out with gardens, open spaces, wide roads, and pleasant neighbourhood shopping centres. Now that shoppers were more mobile, branch provision also seemed unduly generous. Bridlington, for example, had five Co-op shops within a square mile; Hessle, three. Even tiny Newport (population 924) supported two, just a few dozen yards apart along the sole village street. The scope for cutting out 'dead wood' and concentrating on sites suitable for modernisation could no longer be ignored.

And so the blinds came down for the last time at a long string of shops, including some with poetic names like Strawberry Street, Passage Street and Wellington Lane. For the staff, and for those customers moving on to pastures new, it meant the end of a way of life that had remained virtually unaltered for generations. Just as the Gaitskell Report had predicted, not even the mighty Co-op could hold back the forces of change now sweeping through post-war Britain.

Greenwich Avenue. A new way of shopping came to Bilton Grange in 1955, the Co-op being one of Hull's first exponents of supermarkets (Picture by courtesy of CWS).

Another generation of Co-op Branch Managers in the making? The First Hands' Association visit to the CWS Waveney Canneries at Lowerstoft in May 1962.

The new Skyline Department Store in 1963. The silver-coated dome of the Ballroom was said to be the only one of its kind in the world outside the Kremlin (Picture by courtesy of Innes Studios).

CHAPTER SEVEN - A TIME OF UPS AND DOWNS 1964 TO 1980

As the 1960s moved on the Society found the competition facing its core food business steadily hotting up. Names like Savemore Stores, Fine Fare, Goodfellows and Jacksons Discount Food Markets appeared on the scene, bringing to the area some of the keenest prices found anywhere in Britain. The Co-op still had its dividend, of course, but only just. The pulling power of this unique feature was fading away as pressure on profit margins squeezed it firstly to 9d., then to 6d., and later still to 4d. in the £. All the housewife now seemed bothered about was low prices, and she was prepared to shop around to get them.

Still more troubles lay in store for the Society. A half-day strike by 80 Office staff in August 1964, ostensibly in response to Management plans to extend Saturday afternoon working, was widely believed to signify a deeper malaise. The old adage 'no smoke without fire' proved remarkably apt, for by early 1965 an organised campaign was gathering momentum to overthrow the President and entire Board of Directors.

'Bid to topple Hull Co-op chiefs fails.' So ran the *Hull Daily Mail's* dramatic headline, reporting on a special Members' Meeting convened to discuss, in effect, a motion of 'no confidence' in the Society's leaders. Sixty members had petitioned for the debate, after alleged irregularities at the May 1963 Board elections prompted a defeated candidate for the Presidency to sue the Society in the County Court. G&MWU shop-steward Mr. Archie Gemmell had accused the Directors of failing to conduct a proper inquiry into complaints about the conduct of a polling clerk at one of the 22 designated branch shops where members could cast their votes. Accepting evidence that reliable witnesses had seen the clerk feed the ballot box, Judge Norman Harper awarded Mr. Gemmell nominal damages. But he stopped short of declaring the election void since the fraudulently inserted papers could not possibly have swayed the result.

More than 800 members now crowded into the Skyline Restaurant to pass their own judgement on the affair. The controversial proposal was moved by Mr. Fred Hall (Secretary to Hull City Labour Party), seconded by retired Co-op official Mr. Fred Cant, and backed by a group of members calling themselves the Progressives. The heated, indignant gathering approved the motion overwhelmingly. But when the votes were aggregated with those cast earlier at the Branch Meetings in Beverley, Bridlington, Pocklington, Market Weighton and Withernsea, they totalled 602 in favour and 408 against, 70 short of the two-thirds majority required by Rule. Thanks largely to the backwoodsmen of the East Riding, the Board had been saved.

Thus the Directors lived to fight another day. Even so, the episode had brought starkly into the open all the misgivings that many Co-operators had been harbouring about their Society. As well as general anxiety over the declining trading position, more subtle suggestions had been circulating among activists that the £7 million turnover, 2,800 employee business was losing touch with its grass roots membership and breaking away from the wider Labour Movement. The *Humberside Voice*, a local Trades Council paper, in a front page editorial, went so far as to label it 'a sick Society'. Whether or not these views were well-founded (for there were others who insisted that the whole affair had been whipped up purely for political motives), few could deny that the resultant publicity had taken the shine off the Hull Co-op's long-standing reputation for integrity and sound administration.

Though the protestors lost on the day, they had of course merely failed on a technicality. And so the ginger group's campaign continued. An open letter put around before the May 1966 elections likened the Board to a football team and urged members to 'sign on some new players to save the side from relegation'. The Progressives swept into power, capturing seven of the 11

The unique mural facing King Edward Street was designed by Wolverhampton artist Alan Boyson to symbolise Hull's fishing industry. Five men spent eight weeks assembling the one million piece jigsaw of tiny glass cubes on its curved concrete screen (Picture by courtesy of Mr. C.E. Collinson).

The Greatest Free Show in the North: Lord Peddie opening the Family Fare Exhibition, held in the City Hall to commemorate the completion of the new Store. He was accompanied by the CWS (Manchester) Band.

seats and Fred Hall was installed as 'Team Captain' (President).

While all this was going on, the last phase of Jameson Street was completed and all departments finally settled into their intended positions. What became known locally as the Skyline Department Store was officially opened by Sir Leonard Cooke OBE (President of the Co-operative Wholesale Society) on 30th July 1965 in the presence of the city's Lord Mayor (Ald. Miss Annie Major) and many other distinguished guests.

The magnificent new building brought a touch of class to Hull's re-emergent city centre. Its huge silver-coated handkerchief dome - visible for miles around, and massive pale green and brown mural facing King Edward Street, quickly became the shopping centre's most talked-about features. On the balcony a pleasant coffee lounge afforded panoramic views, while at ground level Hull's first ever 'warm air curtain' doorless entrance enticed shoppers into a bright new Skyline Food Hall. The manufactured breeze, designed to keep the heat in and litter and draughts out, must have swept the hat off many an unsuspecting shopper's head as they passed through!

The Store's vital statistics were impressive: Five floors, five entrances, four main staircases, four passenger and three goods lifts, escalators to every level, and a sales area of 146,000 sq.ft. The General Office boasted a 100-foot long banking counter and housed one of the most up-to-date Management suites in the North. Speaking at a dinner to mark the completion, Mr. Arnold Barnes revealed that the Store had cost the Society £1,970,000, less War Damage claims and allowances of £590,000, although an independent valuer had estimated its worth on the open market to be £4 million. Over ten years trade had expanded by 150% but the full potential had yet to be reached, he maintained.

Having added Catering, Petrol sales, Car hire,

Hairdressing, Chiropody, Health foods, Photography and a Wig Boutique to an already wide portfolio of goods and services, the Society was better placed than ever to look after its members' every need. Under the wing of a subsidiary concern (the Skyline Restaurant & Catering Co. Ltd.) it even made a brief foray into the leisure industry, leasing a large hotel and entertainments complex at Primrose Valley near Filey. In hindsight, involvement in risky ventures like these, when the mainstream food business was under such pressure, was a flawed strategy. It seemed to many people that the Society had got its priorities all wrong.

The new Board urgently reviewed everything. But their efforts to turn the business round were hampered by the state of the nation. To redress Britain's economic ills the Government had brought in a wages freeze and tough controls on domestic credit, measures designed to rein back consumer spending. And by 1968 Selective Employment Tax (a tax imposed on service industries by that same supposedly Co-op-friendly Labour Government) was costing the Hull Society £94,000 a year - the equivalent of a 4d. dividend.

Nothing short of major surgery was prescribed: staffing levels were ruthlessly cut; delivery charges imposed on orders; death benefits all but abolished; and uneconomic branches fearlessly axed. For the staff it was an unsettling time but the Directors made it plain they would not shirk their responsibilities to avoid unpopularity. 'The Society has a right to compete on equal terms,' they declared in a pep-talk to members and staff, 'We need your support and confidence. Together we shall weather this storm and look forward to better times.'

The Grocery Department (which still accounted for over 70% of total trade) came in for early attention. A new colour scheme appeared on hitherto dowdy shop fronts. Some stores jettisoned weekly credit, home delivery and

A Wig Boutique - just one of many new services offered by the Society during the 1960s (Picture by courtesy of Innes Studios).

Mr. Fred Hall (Centre) (President of the Hull and East Riding Co-operative Society 1966-74) with Hull City football stars Raich Carter (right) and Ken Wagstaff at the opening of the Skyline Sports Department in 1967 (By courtesy of Ken Kaye).

dividend in favour of extra deep price cuts on everyday lines. Wine shops were opened (the one at Jameson Street aptly named The Skywine!) to tap a burgeoning area of consumer demand.

To aid administrative efficiency, computers were brought in to handle members' shares and streamline ordering routines. There were changes at executive level too: The vacant chief officer post was split, Mr. J.D. Macpherson becoming Secretary (responsible for all administrative matters) and Mr. H. Greening General Manager (to oversee trade development). Mr. Greening arrived from the Rotherham Co-op where he had held a senior post ominously described as 'trouble-shooter'. The Hull Society also became the twelfth in the country to switch over to Co-op Dividend Stamps in place of traditional dividend, which was paid out for the last time in April 1969. Coupled with an aggressive Big-6 Super Savers advertising campaign, these measures reinvigorated the Society's image and turnover started to make healthy advances for the first time in a decade.

Some grey clouds did, however, remain obstinately on the skyline. Members gathering for the Annual Meeting on 22nd April 1969 were quite unprepared for the President's startling announcement that the Society was about to sell and lease back its Central Premises, just four short years after their completion. The deal, with a major insurance company, involved releasing a quarter of the space to British Home Stores while retaining 170,000 sq.ft. on rental for trading and office purposes; in return the Society would receive a capital sum of £2 million.

Some of the funds released would go to pay back external loans, lifting the considerable burden of interest charges and wiping out a £¼ million bank overdraft. £400,000 was to be invested outside the Society as security for the Employees' Pension Fund. As Mr. Greening told

the Press, the balance would be used to improve members' shopping facilities, creating stores on selected sites in the modern image. Work on dividing the Store began in earnest and by the summer of 1970 BHS had opened an attractive variety store and restaurant beneath the symbolic mural on the King Edward Street corner, leaving the Co-op to occupy the Bond Street end and most of the upper floors.

One factor prompting the sale was the declining capital position. Unless rich in reserves generated out of past profits, Co-operatives (with their withdrawable shares) often rely heavily on the propensity of their members to save. In contrast to pre-war days when the Society was awash with funds (mainly undrawn dividends left in accounts), the 1960s had seen its capital base gradually shrink as members drew on their savings to buy consumer goods. And the building societies were fast coming into prominence as a rival home for people's savings.

By designing new investment schemes to attract the longer-term saver, the Society did try hard to arrest the trend. But in November 1969, just when things were looking up on the capital front, the BBC Nationwide TV programme exposed the downfall of the tiny Millom Co-op Society in Cumbria, an area devastated by the closure of the local ironworks. In so doing the broadcast cast doubts on the stability of Co-ops in general. Queues at the banking counter in Jameson Street lengthened as worried investors turned up to withdraw their money 'just in case'. Over the next three weeks, from a total shareholding of £750,000, withdrawals exceeded normal levels by some £40,000. Strenuous protests were made to the BBC and the Prime Minister about 'a slanted and irresponsible attack on the Co-op Movement,' but to no avail; the damage was done. It took two years for the ripple effect to peter out, by which time an attractively-marketed Double Your Money Unit Loan scheme was bringing new capital flowing in again.

Under the 1960s modernisation programme Anlaby Common branch gained an entirely new style of shop front, better suited to self-service.

IT'S NEW! It's CO-OP Cash and Carry
at the
GREENWOOD AVE. SUPERSTORE
JUNCTION OF GREENWOOD AVENUE AND 22nd AVENUE, NORTH HULL ESTATE

OPENS MONDAY, 5th DECEMBER

LOOK at some of our thousands of CUT PRICE LINES

		SAVE
KELLOGGS	1/7½	4d.
QUAKER OATS	1/6	5½d.
P.G. TIPS	1/5½	3½d.
99 TEA	1/5½	3½d.
MARY BAKER Lemon Tops	1/3	6d.
MARY BAKER Butterfly	1/7	4½d.
ROBERTSON'S Golden Shred	1/4½	6d.
ROBERTSON'S Silver Shred	1/4½	6d.
SPRING'S Mincemeat	1/7½	5½d.
SPRING'S Lemon Curd	1/7½	5½d.
HEINZ BEANS	1/1	3d.
HEINZ SOUP Tomato & Veg.	1/-	3d.
KNORR SWISS SOUPS	1/1½	6½d.
KIT-E-KAT	7d.	1½d.
LASSIE	1/4	4½d.
DAZ free MAT offer	2/9½	6½d.
PERSIL	2/9½	6½d.
VIM	10½d.	5½d.
AJAX	10½d.	5½d.
Shoe POLISH Brown & Black	1/-	3d.
RONUK POLISH	1/9	9d.
PLEDGE	4/6	1/6

		SAVE
ZAL FRESH AIR SPRAY	2/11	1/10
PINE DISINFECTANT 26oz.	1/10	1/6
SCOTTIES TISSUES	1/6½	11½d.
SILVIKRIN HAIR CREAM	2/11	7d.
COLGATE SHAVING CREAM	2/6	5d.
STERADENT	2/6	5d.
DELSEY TOILET ROLLS	1/5	11d.
PETAL TOILET ROLLS	1/1½	
EVAPORATED MILK	1/1	3d.
MARVEL	2/-	3d.
FRAY BENTOS CORNED BEEF. 7oz.	3/6	5d.
BOVRIL 8oz.	6/3	5d.
MARMITE 8oz.	3/9	9d.
OXO'S Per doz.	2/2½	9d.
FLETCHER'S PICKLED ONIONS, 16oz.	2/2	8½d.
FLETCHER'S PICKLED CABBAGE, 16oz.	1/6	9d.
RYVITA	10½d.	4d.
PREMIUM CRACKERS	1/-	4½d.
LARD ½lb.	7½d.	5d.
CREAMERY BUTTER Per lb.	2/11	
CANNED PEACHES	1/3½	Tall tin
CANNED APRICOTS	1/1	Tall tin
CANNED PINEAPPLE	1/2	Tall tin
CANNED FRUIT SALAD	1/6	Tall tin
HEINZ BABY FOODS	6½d.	Tin

COME CO-OPERATIVE SHOPPING and SAVE!

MEMBERS PLEASE NOTE!
This is the first of many CASH AND CARRY SUPERSTORES That we plan to open in the future.

SHOPPING HOURS
MONDAY ... 8.30 a.m. to 12.30 p.m.
TUESDAY ... 8.30 a.m. to 5. 0 p.m.
WEDNESDAY 8.30 a.m. to 5. 0 p.m.
THURSDAY ... 8.30 a.m. to 5.30 p.m.
FRIDAY ... 8.30 a.m. to 6. 0 p.m.
SATURDAY ... 8.30 a.m. to 5.15 p.m.

If you are a Town Centre Shopper visit our SKYLINE SUPERSTORE, JAMESON STREET, HULL. Where the same CUT PRICES are available.

HULL & EAST RIDING CO-OPERATIVE SOCIETY LIMITED

The way forward: Cash & Carry trading came to Greenwood Avenue Co-op in 1966. Compare those prices with today's.

More managerial changes occurred in 1970. Mr. Greening resigned and Mr. Frank Izatt was appointed Assistant Secretary. Mr. W.G. Devonald was put in charge of the Food Trades and Mr. Frank Perry became Staff Training Officer. Mr. Perry's brief was to begin in earnest preparing the staff for D-Day - the 15th February 1971 - when every shop would switch over to decimal currency. Hundreds of new cash registers had to be ordered and installed in readiness for this far reaching change.

The Society entered its ninth decade with annual sales of £7 million and 57,000 members. The bright new Co-op colours were going up all over the East Riding as the promised development programme gathered pace. Holland Street - the busiest branch store - was demolished and rebuilt as a supermarket while new premises were converted at Withernsea and Market Weighton. Neither the Bakery nor the Skyline Ballroom were paying their way and so it was decided, not without a great deal of heartsearching, to close them in June 1971. The ballroom had been a worry to the Board from the very start, details of losses frequently being called for at Members' Meetings.

In 1972 the Society rendered a valuable service to local historians and students by depositing its early records and minute books with the Brynmor Jones Library at Hull University, where they can be consulted on request. This was an exceptionally good year. The benefits of modernisation were starting to shine through and, with reserve funds reaching 80% of members' capital, the balance sheet had been restored to health. Plans were now put in hand to turn the unused space above suitable shops into flats for staff and members. But the highlight of 1973 was the opening of a Non-food discount warehouse on Leads Road trading under the Hull Disco banner. In the city that had given birth to the Comet chain of cut-price electrical warehouses, it was an idea that was destined to prove a winner.

County Councillor Fred Hall decided to step down as President at the October elections in 1974. He had served at a critical time in the Society's history and the Half-yearly Report, referring to the onerous measures taken by the Board under his leadership, paid him this tribute: 'These decisions took courage, and it was the quiet determination and strong personality of Fred Hall which enabled the Society to weather the storm of those fateful years and emerge as a strong financially sound organisation.' As his successor members elected Mr. Ernest Cooper, a long-serving Director, former Educational Committee man, and Co-op Party secretary. Like so many of his contemporaries, Mr. Cooper, a Grocery Branch Manager, had spent his entire working life with the Society; he was a Co-op man through and through.

The following year Mr. John Macpherson, the Secretary and Chief Executive Officer, retired after ten years faithful service. It was another 'John' who succeeded him - Mr. J.R. Brown from the Norwich Co-operative Society. Though he found the finances in a fitter state than when 'Mac' had taken over, Mr. Brown still faced an uphill task; the world outside was changing rapidly. Unemployment in the Hull area was 7.2% and rising compared with 4.8% in the wider Yorkshire & Humberside Region. This fact alone made sales growth problematical for the remainder of the decade. The depressed level of consumer spending (especially after the Chancellor raised VAT to 25% on so-called luxury goods in May 1976); more aggressive marketing by national chain stores; and the expansion plans of certain local rivals, all affected turnover in a number of Departments.

Even so, Management were not afraid to try new ideas. At Shannon Road a Frozen Foods Centre was launched to cater for the growing ranks of home-freezer owners. More Disco Stores were opened, plus a handful of Factory Shoe Shops selling 'end of line' footwear at unbeatable prices. The now-ubiquitous plastic card also

Discount shopping - Rugby Street. Despite the new name, the diamond over the door gives away the store's identity as part of the Hull Co-op. Krazy Kuts gave a new lease of life to several older branches in the late 1960s (picture by courtesy of Mr. Reg Lamb, the store manager).

The Hull Co-operative Departmental Managers Association in the 1970s. Shown left to right: Messrs. Charlton (Personnel), Cohen (Textiles), Kaye (Menswear), Perry (Training), Atkins (Store Manager), Bates (Drapery), Henderson (Electrical), Stainton (Coal), Knappett (Furniture), Cuthbertson (Butchery), Izatt (Assistant Secretary), Devonald (Grocery), Collinson (Funerals), Turner (Display), Thompson (Chief Cashier), Macpherson (Secretary), Dobson (Accountant), Anson (Services), Perkins (Traffic) (Picture by courtesy of Mr. C.E. Collinson).

made its debut in 1979, offering members a brand new credit facility. In distribution too there were economies of scale to be won. The Canning Street Grocery Warehouse, with its cramped, multi-floor layout, was hopelessly unsuitable for the latest order-picking and handling techniques. In March 1979 it was declared redundant and all supplies were now trunked direct to the shops in huge transporter vehicles, via the newly-opened M62 motorway, from a large computer-controlled Regional Distribution Centre in the West Riding.

But even with all these streamlining measures, it was clear that trading conditions were likely to remain tough for many years to come. Realisation was dawning too that the balance of advantage was steadily swinging away from the smaller-scale, locally-run retailer. A series of mergers among multiple stores had created some powerful groupings, capable of ploughing vast resources into researching and meeting modern consumer demands at the lowest possible cost.

In its advertising the Society was using the slogan 'Locally Controlled with You in Mind' but it was questionable what real benefits this now offered the shopper. There was little wrong with the range of goods sold, still less with their quality (for which the Co-op had always enjoyed a good reputation). But on price - especially in food - the Hull Co-op was widely perceived as lacking the sharpness of its main rivals. And when East Yorkshire families and pensioners were feeling the pinch, it was 'price' that mattered most when choosing where to shop.

All over Britain Co-operators were coming to realise, reluctantly (since independence is seldom given up lightly), that regional if not national societies offered the best way forward for the Movement. Even so, mergers were far easier to advocate than to achieve. In 1976 plans were mooted for a group society for Yorkshire, which would have allowed 11 societies, including Hull and East Riding, to pool their trading expertise while retaining some local identity. But all came to nothing when a major West Riding society pulled out at the eleventh hour.

However, in 1980, after considering the prospects for continuing to go it alone, the Hull Society Board decided to enter into talks with Co-operative Retail Services Ltd. (CRS) - Britain's largest consumer co-operative - about the possibility of closer union. A new phase of Co-operative history in East Yorkshire was about to begin.

Shopping 1990s style - by car. The Co-operative superstore on Holderness Road, Hull, an example of a 'one-stop' shopping destination.

Smaller Co-operative stores like this one in the Market Place at Hedon are living proof that, with the right location and modern customer services, there is still a place for the community food store.

CHAPTER EIGHT - A NEW BEGINNING: 1980 ONWARDS

In the autumn of 1980 members of the Hull and East Riding Co-op were asked to vote on the most far reaching proposal in their Society's 90 year history. To help them come to a decision the President and Chief Officer issued a pamphlet containing this message:

"After full consideration of our present position and the resources needed to meet ever increasing competition in an unfavourable economic climate, your Board strongly recommend that we join Co-operative Retail Services Limited to provide:
- the guarantee of members' share capital holding at full value,
- better technical and financial resources for the further development of Co-operative trade in the area,
- better buying and marketing facilities with attendant benefits to members,
- better investment facilities for members,
- better prospects of promotion for the staff,
- continued democratic principles in that a committee of 12 members will be elected as the Hull and East Riding Regional Committee of CRS Ltd.

"We would ask members to attend the meetings ...to hear more about the proposal and to support the unanimous recommendation of your Board of Directors."

For the proposal to go ahead, it had to be supported by two-thirds of the members voting at a Special General Meeting. It then had to be confirmed at a further Special Meeting but this time a simple majority would suffice.

Nearly 400 members gathered in the City Hall on Tuesday, 28th October 1980 for the first meeting, the largest turnout seen at a Co-op meeting in Hull for many a year. Understandably, given the importance of the subject matter to their future welfare, a large employee contingent was present; Guild members, retired staff and other activists were also out in force.

The momentous plan generated a lively debate, in which the pros and cons received a thorough airing. It was an emotive occasion, with a number of speakers eloquently championing the view - so obviously felt in the hearts of many - that the Society should think long and hard before giving up its cherished independence. But when the ballot papers were counted, the way ahead was clear. By 196 votes to 56, the requisite majority for a merger had been achieved.

The second meeting, in a packed Co-op Hall on 18th November, endorsed the result by 168 votes to 33. The Hull and East Riding's future now lay in the arms of CRS. The Transfer of Engagements (the legal term for merging all the assets and liabilities) took effect on 1st February 1981. The Hull Co-op added 39,000 members and trade worth £17 million to CRS, which then boasted more than 1.3 million members nationally and an annual turnover approaching £500 million.

Following the changeover, the business continued - initially at least - to be run from Jameson Street as a self-contained Hull and East Riding Region. The Board of Directors became a Regional Committee but was still elected by local Co-op members to look after their interests. Overall policy and direction, however, necessarily passed to the CRS National Board, comprising members chosen by the Regional Committees in all parts of Britain where CRS operates.

However, a survey of Co-op operations in East Yorkshire, and the rapidly changing face of retail shopping, revealed an urgent need to take many difficult decisions. Just how quickly things were moving on had been illustrated by the decision of the Secretary of State for the Environment, in August 1980, to grant planning consent to Asda Stores to build a 51,000 sq.ft. superstore on a green-field site at Bilton. The company's application had originally been rejected by Hull City Council in an attempt to protect the vitality of the city centre and other established local shopping facilities. But with Asda's appeal now won, the city was about to have its first superstore and other major retailers J. Sainsbury and Tesco were also lining up for an onslaught on the area.

Such vast developments were bound to have a drastic impact on shopping habits. Trade would inevitably be drawn away from traditional traders like the Co-op, whose network of comparatively small shops offered little in the way of modern customer comforts. Car parking, for example, was becoming an essential ingredient in the retail offer. Even in Hull (where car ownership has always been well below the national average) the housewife's daily trek to the local shops, armed with her shopping basket, was gradually giving way to the family's weekly trip to a supermarket to fill up the car boot with as many purchases as possible. The Co-op, it seemed, urgently needed to rethink its strategy if it hoped to see its second century.

And so the early 1980s turned out to be the most devastating period in the Society's history, as those stores judged to lack a viable future served their final customers, paid off their staff and shut their doors for the last time. By 1983 the Co-op was conspicuous by its absence from a number of towns and suburban districts where it once held sway. To reduce costs, the Hull and East Riding Region had also been absorbed into an expanded Yorkshire CRS, administered from Barnsley.

The city of Hull had been especially taken aback by the news which confronted it on 10th May 1982: 'Hull Co-op Store is Closing Down - Shock as over 100 lose jobs' screamed the *Hull Daily Mail's* front-page, revealing that the main Jameson Street Department Store was scheduled to close in three months time. According to the report, the bombshell announcement came within weeks of CRS losing a battle for a new superstore site on former British Rail land in West Hull to Sainsbury's.

Mr. John Hewitt (the CRS Regional General Manager for Yorkshire) spelt out the reasons behind it: Firstly, the Store had been unprofitable for some time and would have needed over £1 million spending on it just to bring it up to present-day standards. It had of course since 1969 been leased from a major insurance company. With a rent review imminent, the landlords were pressing for a hefty increase to recompense them for some 14 years of rapid inflation, which would have rendered it even less viable. Yet another problem related to the Store's layout. The 1970 'carve up' had left the Co-op with the lion's share of the upper floors while giving BHS a bigger slice of premium ground floor selling space. In our fast-moving modern age, it seemed people were becoming less inclined to wander leisurely from floor to floor to do their shopping.

There is no doubt that Co-operative pride took a severe knock with the closure. Words of shock and sadness seemed to be on everyone's lips when asked for a reaction to the news. Mr. Ron Lang, secretary to Hull Chamber of Trade, summed up local feeling well: 'The Co-op has been established in the city for so long that it is difficult to imagine the centre without it.' For many Co-operative die-hards it was effectively the end of the old Hull Co-op as they had known it. For the staff, many of whom had years of loyal service behind them, it was a particularly cruel blow, coming at a time when jobs in the Hull Travel to Work Area were especially hard to find.

Throughout the summer shoppers snapped up some unbelievable bargains as the stock was systematically cleared out. At the banking counter there were daily scenes, as one observer put it, 'reminiscent of the Wall Street crash' as members queued in huge number to cash in their share books before the appointed closure day - Saturday 7th August 1982. As CRS shares are backed by massive reserves, there was no question of anyone losing any money. People just couldn't face the inconvenience of dealing by post with a remote office in Barnsley, or with one of the remaining Co-op shops. For some the amount of money involved was insignificant; their action was simply a way of registering their feelings at the loss of their much-loved store.

During this gloomy period, there were at least some bright spots for Co-operators to focus on. The Co-operative Women's Guild celebrated a century of endeavour with a well-supported rally attended by the city's Lord Mayor. The Co-operative Bank sounded an upbeat note by moving to prestigious new premises next door to Marks & Spencer's. Co-op Travel and Co-op Optical Services both moved out of Jameson Street into shop units nearby, bringing them into greater public prominence. And Co-operation in general took a step forward in 1985 when a local Co-operative Development Agency was set up, charged with encouraging and supporting the formation of worker co-ops on Humberside.

The year 1985 also saw a far reaching overhaul of CRS administration. A new-style Humberside Regional Committee (one of 25 across the country) was created to represent members. Co-operators from Hull and the East Riding now joined up with those from Scunthorpe and Grimsby, and Members' Meetings began to alternate between north and south of the Humber.

CRS also adopted a set of 'social objectives' in order to spell out its obligations - and Co-operative values - to its customers, members, employees and the wider community. As Co-op members were becoming increasingly vociferous at Members' Meetings on issues of public concern, the idea captured the mood of the age perfectly. Indeed it was just such member pressure that encouraged the CRS Board to ban South African goods from the Society's shops while the apartheid system prevailed, a move later copied by other retailers.

Similar pressure later led to a decision to de-list those children's toys that glorify war or violence. Another area where CRS was swift to take an enlightened stance was in protecting the environment. The first retailer to ban harmful CFCs from its aerosols and packaging materials, the Co-op was also in the vanguard of informative product labelling and concern for animal welfare, and an early convert to lead-free fuel for its vehicle fleet, to quote just a few examples of what might be termed 'responsible retailing'.

The Society's search for a site on which to build a large store to serve the next generation of Co-operators finally bore fruit in late-1987. Hull Kingston Rovers, one of the city's top Rugby League clubs, faced with the need to meet tough new safety requirements in the aftermath of the Bradford City fire disaster, were looking to sell their Craven Park home on Holderness Road and move to a new purpose-built stadium at Greatfield. CRS fended off competition from another major retailer to acquire the entire site, together with an adjacent disused bus depot. A local firm was appointed to handle the development, which received planning consent in 1988.

Rovers moved out at the close of their 1988/9 playing season and demolition of the old stands, together with the massive 'tote board' (a familiar East Hull landmark, used for the greyhound racing), began immediately. By the end of 1989 construction work on a 75,000 sq.ft. superstore was well under way. The project received an early vote of confidence from local people when the recruitment notices in the Press attracted no fewer than 3,500 applicants for the 350 new jobs on offer.

Opening on 25th September 1990, Hull's flagship Co-op Leo's Superstore featured a 20 check-out supermarket, 100-seater coffee shop, children's play area, several concessionary shops and parking for over 600 cars. In due course an automatic banking kiosk, Post Office

The Co-operative Funeral Home on Boothferry Road was opened by the Deputy Lord Mayor of Hull, Councillor Mrs Marjorie Smelt, on 30th October 1987 to serve the western parts of the city.

The Homeworld Co-operative 'megastore' which opened in 1998 at Kingswood District Centre, North Hull.

and Co-op Travelcare branch were added to the range of facilities to create a true one-stop shopping experience. The store quickly established itself as a popular weekly shopping destination for thousands of families.

A question often asked was, 'why Leo's?' The story goes that CRS bought its first superstore site from a garage man who had kept a lion tethered up outside his premises. Leo the lion was such an established figure in his South Wales community that he provided an ideal name for a King among superstores! In 1995 the store was one of many nationwide to be 're-badged' Co-operative Pioneer to highlight its unique ownership and commitment to the enduring values of its founding fathers.

Sadly, the initial success turned out to be short-lived, proving that nothing stands still in today's world of retailing. Despite the store's many excellent features, by 1998 the volume of competition locally was providing customers with a very wide choice and its fortunes had taken a dip. The market for superstore shopping was becoming increasingly dominated by a small number of operators whose high profit levels enabled them to invest heavily in powerful marketing campaigns, introduce a variety of innovations, and pay astronomical prices to acquire new sites.

With the prospect of even more competition to come, the CRS Board reluctantly concluded that concentrating on what its Food Division does best - running smaller supermarkets and well-located convenience stores - rather than trying to turn back an irreversible tide, offered the best strategy for future Co-operative success. Selling the Hull Pioneer store on favourable terms to an established superstore operator would provide funds for a new development and refurbishment programme as well as safeguard the jobs of all the staff. Accordingly, the store was disposed of to the Morrison's chain in September 1998.

This policy has already benefited the other East

Yorkshire communities where CRS has a successful trading presence. The Co-operative Food Stores at Howden, North Ferriby, Hedon, Market Weighton and Pocklington have all been extensively re-equipped to offer a wider stock range, better layout and more convenient opening hours. Each store now receives a daily replenishment of fresh and chilled foods, ensuring that everything on sale is in peak condition and minimising the need to tie up expensive capital in backroom stock.

The Co-operative Funeral Home on Holderness Road is shortly to be rebuilt, to provide an even higher standard of bereavement care. Large-scale Co-operative Non-food trading has returned to the Hull area after an absence of 15 years. A 45,000 sq.ft. Homeworld Co-operative megastore - selling everything for the home under one roof - has opened at the Kingswood district centre on the city's northern outskirts. One irony here is that a key factor in the decision to develop on this site was the presence of an Asda superstore and a range of other customer-pulling stores like Boots the Chemists. The Society has carefully researched customers' needs to offer an altogether different shopping and leisure experience. And it has done so with some style. At the very cutting edge of retailing, the new Homeworld concept is shattering old preconceptions of the Co-op. 'To see the look of amazement on first time visitors' faces is to witness a real "wow" factor at work,' according to one senior manager. The store's launch in August 1998 surpassed all expectations, with shoppers coming from as far away as York, Goole, Scunthorpe and Scarborough.

Developments like these are all part of a continuous evolution of trading strategy, as the 'Shop for the People' strives to satisfy today's discerning consumers and advances with confidence towards the year 2000.

HULL CO-OPERATIVE SOCIETY LIMITED
TABLE OF PROGRESS

Year	Sales £	Members	Share Capital £	Reserve Funds £	Rate of Dividend s./d.
1890	1,421	260	212	-	-
1895	5,809	649	1,092	46	1/6
1900	35,010	2,017	7,158	351	1/7¾
1905	176,476	9,067	40,278	2,218	1/11
1910	301,089	15,347	80,958	4,367	1/8
1915	505,502	23,103	158,557	6,861	1/6½
1920	963,623	32,202	371,197	13,286	1/-
1925	977,651	32,800	392,259	5,203	9d.
1930	1,234,093	40,000	545,044	18,194	1/5
1935	1,433,482	50,000	784,988	46,700	1/4
1940	2,053,861	60,000	1,002,936	63,238	1/3
1945	2,281,924	60,000	1,425,241	81,900	1/3
1950	4,126,860	64,300	1,372,453	160,682	1/4 & 1/3
1955	6,108,360	70,000	1,531,460	250,900	1/- & 9d.
1960	7,808,714	74,790	1,506,289	290,400	1/-
1965	7,898,636	81,802	1,476,572	198,585	6d.
1970	7,035,369	57,194	598,923	364,571	-
1975	13,095,924	54,498	640,876	608,227	-
1980	16,700,250*	39,315+	794,740	n/a	-

* estimated
+ after pruning the Register to remove unused accounts

In 1995 the Humberside Region of CRS had Sales of some
£50 million, Share Capital of £3 million and more than 54,000
members.

APPENDIX A: OWNED BY THE PEOPLE WE SERVE

In its heyday the Hull and East Riding Co-op boasted a mass membership of some 80,000. One of the first things most women did, on setting up a home of their own, was join the Co-op (generally pronounced *Corp* by Hull folk or, in its expanded form, *Cor-per-ay-tiv*). Being a member meant being a part-owner of the business, entitling you to share in the profits - the famous Co-op dividend.

Unlike companies, which reward their shareholders according to how many shares they hold, Co-op dividend is based on members' purchases. This distinction reflects the Rochdale Pioneers' belief that it was more equitable to reward a member's loyalty than their personal wealth.

Dividend on Purchases.

Twice every year, after working out its trading profit, the Hull Co-op would declare a dividend of so much 'in the £' of members' purchases. To thousands of East Yorkshire families, struggling to eke out their meagre income, the 'Co-op divi' was a life-line. Often it paid for the children's new shoes and winter coats, or made it possible to have Christmas treats or a holiday by the sea. By way of illustration, when the dividend was 1/6d. in the £, a family spending £2 a week at the Co-op collected £7/16/- a year - the 1930s equivalent of two weeks' earnings (roughly £400 in today's terms).

Members with less pressing needs could save their divi in their share account. In this way people with normally little money to spare often managed to put by a handy nest-egg. And thanks to the Co-op, dreams were sometimes fulfilled, such as owning a first motor car or laying down a deposit on a house.

For the Society, however, before the computer age, administering the dividend was both costly and laborious. The spendings of thousands of customers had to be carefully recorded and each one's correct entitlement calculated, while minimising any opportunity for fraud. From 1918 onwards the Society used what was known as the Gledhill Patent Till system. Members making purchases were given little printed checks which they had to fasten, one after another, on to sheets of gummed paper. When full, the checks had to be totted up, a little ritual nearly always delegated to the youngsters of the family. Years of reckoning up Mum's check sheets, without the aid of a pocket calculator, perhaps help to explain why today's older generation is so adept at mental arithmetic.

The check sheet was then handed in at the Store where, in similar fashion, a practised assistant could accurately verify the total. A red check bearing that value was now fixed to the bottom of a new sheet, to be filled up as before. At the half-year end members exchanged their last sheet for a Final Receipt slip showing what they had spent in the period. From the copies of these slips the Office worked out how much dividend each member was due.

By the 1940s the Hull Society was regularly paying out £400,000 a year in dividend, a valuable sum in those days. The Board came under great pressure to maintain the rate, which was widely viewed as a barometer of its health. But, as trading conditions altered, some fluctuations were unavoidable. In the weeks leading up to its declaration, the sense of anticipation was immense. 'Will our divi be up or down this time?' was the number one topic on every member's lips. One Saturday morning, Ron Jaques, the newly-installed Branch Manager at Barmston Street, found his shop filling up with regulars, waiting for the Office to 'phone through with the vital news. When the call finally came it bore grim tidings - the rate was down from 1/1d. to 9d. in the £. Ron took up his whitewash brush and went outside to paint it up on the window, with the restless crowd jostling all around him. No sooner had he started to describe a big round 9 on the glass than a threatening voice piped up: 'You've missed off the shilling!' Ron decided to beat a

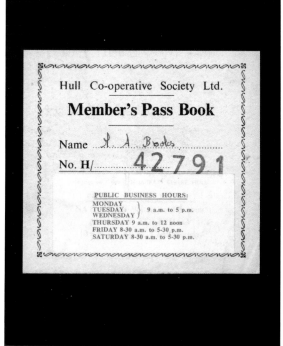

Gledhill Tills were used in all Hull Co-op shops until 1971. To register a sale you placed a metal 'pen' into the slot next to the price, pulled down the sliding bar and pressed a trigger that printed a check. A turn of the handle then caused the cash drawer to spring open.

A Co-op Pass Book, showing the oft-quoted Share Number. Although most members tended to be housewives, some families had both adults in membership and an arrangement that, say, groceries went on Father's number and drapery on Mother's.

HULL CO-OPERATIVE SOCIETY, LTD.
SPECIAL NOTICE
PAYMENT OF
DIVIDEND

Members are requested to note the following arrangements for the payment of Dividend, and to avoid the Week-end crush by visiting the

Offices : 26 JARRATT ST., HULL,

on the days their respective Numbers have been specially allocated

which are as follows :—

Nos.	1 to 15,000	Tues.	Nov. 8th
,,	15,001 to 30,000	Wed.	,, 9th
,,	30,001 to 50,000	Thurs.	,, 10th
,,	50,001 upwards	Friday	,, 11th
Any numbers	- -	Sat.	,, 12th

SPECIAL HOURS FOR THIS WEEK ONLY 9 a.m. to 4 p.m.

The Authority on the back of the Dividend Warrant must be completed when the member cannot attend personally

17th October 1960   A. BARNES,
R 8000 10-60   General Manager and Secretary

To cope with the crowds at dividend time, members were allocated special days according to their Share Number.

hasty retreat, in the sure belief that he was about to be lynched.

The eagerly-awaited pay-out came in May and in November (just in time for Christmas shopping). Dividend Week always drew huge queues to Head Office, where the staff needed super-human stamina as upwards of 12,000 members filed past the counter. After collecting their cash, housewives generally made a bee-line for the Jameson Street Store. But the crowds in the town with extra money in their purses and wallets rarely went unnoticed by rival traders, Bladon's, Hammond's, and Thornton-Varley's. Invariably they arranged a Sale to coincide with Divi Week. The Co-operators' loyalty was tested to breaking-point as these firms vied with each other to lure them away from the Stores.

Dividend was also paid out at the country and seaside branches. At Beverley, two trusty clerks from Jarratt Street - usually Bill Oxley and Reg Kemp - would set up a trestle-table at the back of the Drapery Department for a day. It was cleverly arranged so that members had to pass the full run of well-stocked counters on their way out. According to one observer: 'So many people came along that the queue snaked round the corner and right down Toll Gavel. People were staring out of bus windows open-mouthed wondering what on earth was going on.'

Divi-time could be a godsend if there was surplus stock. While touring Scotland on holiday, Mr. Marshall was once talked into buying a job lot of safety razors. He must have been caught 'off guard', for S.M. was normally the most cautious of men. The razors turned out to be a kind that Hull folk were unfamiliar with and the Store just couldn't shift them. After much head-scratching over how to turn them back into cash, a novel marketing idea was hit upon. An assistant went up and down the divi queue praising the virtues of this 'amazing new product'. Confronted with such an offer, lady members leaving the counter with ready money just couldn't resist treating their menfolk and the razors disappeared like the proverbial hot cakes.

Talking of cakes, Jean Oxley recalls an exciting time at the Office: 'It happened to be Divi Week when VE Day was declared. All the shops closed for the celebrations and so we missed a day's payment. When we reopened the next day it was Any Share Number and you couldn't move in Kingston Square for the crowds. The Bakery had made lots of sponge cakes, all decorated for VE Day, and so we caught them on the way out, with cash in their hands. Everybody bought a sponge cake to celebrate Victory!'

When Resale Price Maintenance was abolished in the 1960s, traders' profit margins were squeezed as never before. The days of huge dividends were over. When the rate slipped to 2d. in the £, shoppers lost interest. In an age of relative affluence, people were attracted by the instant cut prices of the discount stores and less inclined to bother queueing twice a year at the Co-op. So, on 26th August 1968, the old way was abandoned and Co-op Dividend Stamps were introduced into all Departments. Customers received one stamp for every 1/- (5p) they spent, to save in a book which, when full, was worth 10/- (50p) in goods or 8/- (40p) in cash. Members investing stamp books in their share account were given an extra bonus.

Dividend Stamps were perhaps more akin to the 'trading stamps' then in vogue than a true profit-sharing scheme. For one thing they were issued to all customers, not just Co-op members. Consequently, the enrolment of new members fell at a stroke. Next, the rate of return was no longer directly related to Society profits. And stamps could be 'spent' as soon as a stamp book was full. So the excitement of Dividend Weeks was no more. But, though the return was only modest, Dividend Stamps did prove remarkably popular and were only phased out in 1992.

Now that the technology exists to streamline

administration, interest in traditional Co-op dividend has revived. Gone are the paper checks and gummed sheets; in their place, a slick plastic Co-operative Shareholder card which also serves as a cheque guarantee and credit card. The card is swept through the till and the purchases are accumulated by computer, dividend being credited to the share account annually. With slimmer profit margins on food, the scheme has so far been restricted to Non-food stores but extending it has not been ruled out. It has certainly given a new impetus to Co-op membership.

Though dividend was seen as the most important, the Hull Co-op did offer its members a number of other benefits:

Share, Loan and Small Savings Accounts.

Many East Yorkshire people regarded their black Co-op Share Book as their bank book and a natural home for any savings they had. Members were expected to take up at least £2 in share capital, either in cash, accumulated dividend or both. A £2 share-holder was entitled to vote at Society Meetings and help to choose the President, Management Committee, Educational Committee and Co-operative Congress delegates.

Share capital earned only a modest rate of interest, though regular purchasing members did enjoy a preferential return. For non-members, Loan accounts were also offered, but without conferring any voting rights.

Small Savings accounts - often referred to as the Penny Bank - introduced children to the habit of saving and were popular for *Diddle-ums* (local parlance for Christmas Clubs). Depositors could pay in up to £2 at a time at the Office or any Grocery branch and hold a maximum of £50.

Death Benefit Scheme.

Depending on a member's average purchases,

the Society invariably paid a grant when a Co-op member or his/her spouse or child died. Its value increased by 50% if the Co-op was entrusted with the funeral. Normal benefits continued throughout the last war, when 367 Co-op members lost their lives. But after the State Death Grant was introduced, they were restricted to those ineligible for full State Grant. A member spending £1 a week at the Co-op in, say, 1963 qualified for £7/16/- on the death of a husband, or £5/4/- on the death of a wife.

Sick Room Equipment.

The Society kept a stock of bed pans, Bath chairs, crutches and other aids, which needy members could hire for just a few coppers. This useful scheme, managed by a small Committee and run by the ladies of the Women's Guild for over 50 years, was eventually superseded by State health care. Through the Society members could also book a stay at a Co-operative Convalescent Home.

Anniversary Cakes.

In 1934 the Hull Co-op became arguably the first in the country to make the unusual gesture of presenting a complimentary cake, made and decorated in the Society's Bakery, to members celebrating their Golden or Diamond Wedding Anniversary.

Fifty Years Membership.

From 1940 (the Society's Golden Jubilee year) the Management Committee decided to award a £5 gift to all loyal purchasing members when they attained fifty years of continuous membership. The award was increased to £20 worth of Co-op Gift Vouchers in 1974 until the scheme ended in 1981.

Involvement in the Society.

Any Co-op member eligible under the Rules could be nominated to serve on the Management

Committee (Board of Directors) or the Educational Committee and, if elected, play a fulfilling role in helping to run the Society.

Elections took place once a year at the Members' Meetings. At one time there were also polling stations at the General Office and out-of-town branch shops. Often the elections were hotly contested and it was not unknown for pressure groups to field a 'slate' of candidates and issue a manifesto similar to the practice in local government. In the 1960s a Progressives ginger group was active in the Society. This in turn spawned a breakaway group known as the '69 Group' led by Councillor Fred Hall.

Employees serving as directors are quite common in the Co-operative Movement. In the Hull Society no Board places were reserved for workers as such; they took their chance in the elections alongside other customer-members. But, from 1953, the Rules stipulated that worker directors could never form a majority of the Board.

Co-op members can still take part in the work of Co-operative Retail Services by attending Members' Meetings and seeking election to the Humberside Regional Committee or Humberside Member Relations Committee. Regional Committtes are at the heart of the Society's democratic process. By visiting shops, receiving reports, raising questions and bringing matters to the attention of the Board, they monitor its performance and represent the views of members at a local level. They also elect the national Board of Directors. Member Relations Committees help CRS, in all kinds of imaginative ways, to build links with its members and the wider community and organise many in-store events. Serving on these Committees is enjoyable and today's members tend to be every bit as passionate about Co-operation as their forebears! They receive training, support and a small fee for their efforts.

As a tribute to their dedicated service, a list of Co-operators who have served on the principal committees since 1890 appears on the next page.

Members who have served on the Management Committee (Board of Directors) of the Hull Co-operative Society Ltd.*, and/or the Humberside Regional Committee of Co-operative Retail Services Ltd.

Algar, T. 1896-1912
Allott, +
Anderson, G.P. 1895-6
Andrew, G.T. 1911-3
Anfield, T.R. 1898-1901

Bartlett, H. +
Barton, Mrs E. 1922-34
Bateman, Mrs E.M. 1961-5
Bateman, T.
Bayes, S.J. 1994-
Bayford, W. 1901-11
Bell, J.T. 1969-94
Bentley, F.C. 1967-89
Berridge, C. + -1898
Boyes, W. 1905-29
Boynton, A.J. 1898-1922
Bradley, +
Brewer, J.A. 1958-61
Broadberry, +
Broadwell, Mrs J. 1975-85
Brown, T. 1919-22
Brunning, G. 1961-7
Brusby, W. 1947-8
Butterfield, W.H. 1890- +
Butterworth, J. 1895-8

Cant, F.
Chinnery, Miss A.E. 1975-7
Clappison, Mrs M. 1937-43
Clark, J.H. 1902-6;1910-9
Clarke, J. 1913-21
Clarke, S. 1961-6
Clayton, J.F. 1919-20
Cooling, W. + -1894
Cooper, E.H. 1956-68;1970-87
Cooper, Mrs M.E. 1982-7
Couling, G. +
Cross, Mrs B. 1963-7

Dawson, Mrs A.F. 1979-82
Day, F.W. 1914-24
Dearing, H.K. 1976-
Deyes, W. 1930-46
Downs, J.W. 1945-58
Drewry, M.A. + -1894

Edmond, Mrs E. 1900-1;1913-27
Elliott, Mrs C. 1934-46
Emblem, E. 1907-13
Emblen, J.C. 1923-4;1927-8
Enderby, Mrs K. 1966-70;1972
Evans, Mrs J. 1901-3

Fallowfield, G. 1964-6
Farrah, R.H. 1905-10
Ferguson, W. 1900
Fergusson, A. 1900-16
Fergusson, A.E. 1936-55
Firth, G. +
Foord, J.H. 1960-1;1966-73
Fulcher, J. 1890- +
Fussey, G.D. 1956-60

Gaunt, +
Gemmell, A.S. 1956;1958-63;1966-70
Giles, S. 1968-79
Goring, Mrs B. 1976-83
Goring, Mrs L. 1973-5
Gray, Mrs N. 1947-8
Gray, R.W. 1959-66
Green, Mrs K. 1972-6

Hagues, H. + -1896
Haines, G. 1970-9
Hall, F. 1966-74
Hall, T.G. 1898-1929
Hallett, W. + -1900
Harper, W. 1967-9
Harrison, J.J. 1896-1900
Hebb, Miss P.M. 1957-61
Henderson, F.W. 1985-
Holmes, F. 1926-29
Holmes, Miss M. 1974-7
Horton, W. + -1894
Howarth, W. 1892-96

Ireland, D.A. 1890-6;1903-7
Ireland, W.D. +

Jackson, - 1897
Jackson, F.A. 1949-56
Jackson, Mrs G.M. 1974-6
James, J.M. 1890-4
Johnson, +
Johnson, F. 1956-63

King, N.F. 1958
Kirk, W.H. 1930-61
Knight, H. 1912-8;1921-2

Lamb, S. +
Lancaster, R. 1922-3
Leaf, R. +
Leaf, J.S. 1890-6
Lecuas, A.F. 1963-5
Ledger, A. 1931-42;1946-9;1954-6

Leonard, J. +
Lickes, J. 1901-14
Logan, D. 1969-77
Longden, 1897-8

McTurk, +
Mail, Mrs M.J. 1941-6
Maltby, Mrs J.L. 1953-61
Millington, W.G. 1890
Moulds, C. 1890- +
Morris, G.E. + -1898
Morris, H.J. +
Moxley, A. + -1892

Oates, Mrs C.L. 1941-5;1947-59
Oxley, Mrs J. 1970-6

Parker, T. 1902-4
Payling, W.J. 1890- +
Pearson, C. 1977-84
Peddie, J.M. 1942-7;1948-54 @
Peel, A. 1929-41
Pond, W.J. 1896-1906
Price, E. 1920-9

Ramsay, T.S. 1935-57
Randerson, A.E. 1944;1946-8;1960-4
Reed, S. 1959-66
Rice, J. 1900-29
Robertshaw, L. 1890
Robinson, I. 1922-41 %
Russell, J. 1896-7

Saunders, W.H. 1959-68
Scarborough, J. 1978-80
Senior, Mrs N. 1977-86
Seymour, T. 1890- +
Sheppardson, Mrs T. 1929-31
Skelton, Mrs I. 1943-54
Slater, Mrs A. 1910-12;1914-29
Smelt, B. 1984-
Smith, Mrs E. 1970-2
Smith, J.E. 1980-
Smith, W. 1967-9
Sorrie, J.T. 1964-7
Stark, A. 1923-31;1934-7
Stead, T.B. 1890
Stone, H.J. 1930-8

Taylor, M. 1890- +
Taylor, T.C. 1890- +
Teall, E.S. 1949-56
Thirsk, S. 1930-53 %

Thompson, J.S. 1912

Walker, F.C. 1952-9
Walker, Mrs L. 1955-61;1965-70
Walmsley, C. 1969-71
Walters, Mrs N. 1948-58
West, G.W. 1908-11
White, Mrs M.A. 1916-34
Whiteley, D.E. 1967-9
Whitelock, N.S. 1966-74
Wilburn, K. 1961-6
Winter, H. 1924-7
Winter, Mrs M.L. 1927-47
Wright, F.W. 1948-9
Wright, J.F. 1946-7
Woods, Mrs E.M. 1976-86

Note:
* Name of society changed to Hull and East Riding Co-operative Society Ltd. in 1962. Society joined Co-operative Retail Services Ltd. in 1981.

+ pre-1894 (records not found).

@ Also a Director of CWS, CIS and CPBS.
% Also member of Central Board, Co-operative Union Ltd.

Presidents of the Hull Co-operative Society Ltd.

Millington, W.G. 1890
James, J.M. 1890-1
Ireland, D.A. 1891-5
Butterworth, J. 1895-8
Anfield, T.R. 1898-1901
Boynton, A.J. 1901-22
Boyes, W. 1922-9
Robinson, I. 1929-36 %
Peel, A. 1936-41
Kirk, W.H. 1941-61
Johnson, F. 1961-3
Gray, R.W. 1964-6
Hall, F. 1966-74
Cooper, E.H. 1974-81

Chairmen of CRS Regional Committee:

Cooper, E.H. 1981-3
Bell, J.T. 1983-5;1986-94
Smith, J.E. 1997-

Co-op members 'minding their own business'. The Management Committee and Officials on the platform for the Society's half-yearly meeting in the Metropole Hall, Hull in 1940.

Cover of a Quarterly Report to Members.

HULL CO-OPERATIVE SOCIETY LIMITED

Established 1890.

The Society's Modern Grocery, Provision and Confectionery Branch.

HOWDEN, Yorks.

The 192nd

QUARTERLY REPORT

of the Management and Educational Committees

For the three months ended June 4th, 1938.

Registered Offices · · · · 26 Jarratt Street, Hull.

A1337/38.   HULL PRINTERS LIMITED.

APPENDIX B: AROUND THE DEPARTMENTS

GROCERY DEPARTMENT

Grocery (including Greenfruit) Managers:

H.K. Whitehead	J.H. Sharpe	T. Bowden
J.A. Wilde	W.R. Hutchinson	F.A. Jackson
S. Bentley	J.M. Whitehead	G.S. Earley
W. Starks	C.H. Davidson	W.G. Devonald (Food Trades Officer)
T. Yates	H.J. Stone	

Grocery and Butchery Branches:

No.	Branch		Grocery	Butchery
	201 Hessle Road		1890-1891	
1	11 Wilton Terrace		1890-1905	
	94-6 Holderness Road		1905-1969	
2	188 Waterloo Street		1895-1897	
	189-91 Waterloo Street	$	1897-1971	1922-1964
3	257 Hessle Road		1896-1899	
	398 Hessle Road		1899-1907	
	363-7 Hessle Road	$	1907-1976	1915-1974
4	438-40 Anlaby Road		1898-1988	
5	37 De Grey Street		1900-1965	
6	268-70 Holderness Road		1901-1982	1922-1982
7	205-9 Hawthorn Avenue		1901-1981	1915-1970
8	155 Hessle Road		1901-1908	
	61 Hessle Road		1908-1964	
9	72-4 Londesborough Street		1902-1968	1922-1963
10	42 Great Passage Street		1902-1964	
11	592-4 Hessle Road		1903-1965	1927-1964
12	71-3 Princes Avenue		1903-1970	1934-1983
13	294-6 Stoneferry Road		1904-1970	1936-1968
14	Hessle, Gladstone Street		1905-1925	
	" Northgate		1925-1982	1925-1971
15	357 Hedon Road		1905-1941*	
16	74-6 New Cleveland Street		1905-1970	1922-1963
17	Cottingham, 2 Exeter Street		1906-1967	
18	Bridlington, 76 Quay Road		1908-1968	1922-1968
19	195-9 New Bridge Road		1908-1969	1929-1964
20	69-71 Wellington Lane		1908-1965	1930-1964
21	73-5 Cholmley Street		1909-1981	1936-1968
22	179-83 Newland Avenue		1909-1968	1915-1973
23	Howden, Churchside		1911-1937	
	" Market Place		1937-	
24	Bridlington, Chapel Street		1913-1967	
	" King Street		1967-1977	
	" Chapel Street		1977-1982	
25	92-3 Barmston Street		1913-1965	
26	65-9 Endymion Street		1913-1972	1929-1969
27	77-9 Charles Street		1914-1968	1922-1964
28	1-2 Clarence Street		1914-1928	
20	2 Strawberry Street		1928-1965	1928-1963
29	76-8 Chanterlands Avenue		1914-1982	1928-1982
30	Marfleet Avenue		1914-1971	1929-1963
31	445-51 Anlaby Road	$	1914-1981	1922-1973
32	South Cave, Market Place		1914-1982	
33	Withernsea, 201 Queen Street		1915-1971	1926-1972
	" 211 Queen Street		1971-1982	

No.	Branch		Grocery	Butchery
34	184 Hessle Road		1915-1925	
	152-4 Hessle Road		1925-1967	
35	93 Great Thornton Street		1915-1964	
36	506 Holderness Road		1915-1969	
37	Newport, Main Street		1916-1963	
38	Wallingfen, Canal Side		1916-1975	
39	Bridlington, 41 High Street	$	1919-1986	1936-1986
40	Hedon, Market Place		1919-	1925-1988
41	Cottingham, Hallgate		1918-1937	
	" 177 Hallgate		1937-1987	1937-1970
42	Bridlington, West Street		1920-1967	1922-1967
43	Flamborough, Dog & Duck Square		1920-1969	
44	41-5 Sculcoates Lane		1921-1941*	1930-1941*
45	817-9 Hessle Road		1921-1976	
46	Hornsea, 140 Newbegin		1921-1976	
47	817-21 Holderness Road		1926-1976	1926-1971
48	Jameson Street, Arcade		1923-1941*	1923-1927
	" Skyline Pantry		1963-1982	1963-1982
49	75 Bentley Grove		1927-1973	1927-1966
50	245 Anlaby Road		1929-1971	
51	550 Beverley High Road		1929-1936	
	580-2 Beverley High Road		1936-1971	1936-1969
52	Beverley, Register Square	@	1929-1982	@ 1929-1982
53	" Grovehill Road	@	1929-1982	1937-1981
54	226-30 Boothferry Road		1929-1986	1929-1985
55	949-53 Spring Bank West		1930-1982	1930-1980
56	284-6 Southcoates Lane		1930-1986	
57	46 New Bridge Road		1937-1970	
58	316 Marfleet Lane		1932-1993	
59	260 Greenwood Avenue	$	1934-1981	1934-1974
60	185 Gillshill Road		1934-1981	
61	734-6 Spring Bank West		1935-1967	1938-1967
62	Willerby		1935-1967	
63	Anlaby Common		1935-1982	1935-1973
64	1133 Hessle High Road		1935-1970	1935-1968
65	North Ferriby, High Street		1935-	
66	First Avenue, North Hull Estate		1937-1979	1937-1970
67	Hessle, Northfield		1937-1969	1937-1968
68	252-4 Wold Road		1937-1982	1937-1980
69	Bricknell Avenue		1937-1984	1937-1981
70	Bridlington, Queensgate		1938-1980	1938-1980
71	148-152 County Road South		1939-1975	1939-1973
72	660 Anlaby Road (Wilkinson's)		1945-1971	
73	40 Ellerby Grove (Curson Bros.)		1945-1981	
74	453 Endike Lane (Hargreaves)		1945-1984	

		Grocery	Butchery
75	308 Beverley Road (Taylor's)	1945-1971	
76	455 Endike Lane (Dawson's)	1947-1984	
77	Hessle, Gisburn Road	1954-1967	1954-1967
		1969-1979	
78	436 Marfleet Lane	1955-1976	
79	Greenwich Avenue	1955-	1955-1981
80	Patrington, Market Place	1956-1976	1956-1963
81	Anlaby, 11 Hull Road	1956-1969	
82	Pocklington, Market Street @	1956-	1958-1985
83	Bishop Wilton @	1956-1969	
84	Stamford Bridge @	1956-1965	
85	Wilberfoss @	1956-1968	
86	Willerby, 149 Kingston Road	1957-1981	
87	Winchester Avenue	1957-1981	
88	803 Hotham Road South	1958-1982	
89	84-6 Shannon Road	1959-1988	1959-1988
90	Elm Bridge Parade	1959-	1959-198?
91	Little Weighton	1961-1969	
92	224-6 Orchard Park Road	1962-1980	
93	Market Weighton, York Road @	1963-1974	
	" Market Place	1972-	
94	Holme upon Spalding Moor @	1963-1972	
95	Seaton Ross, The Cross @	1963-1969	
96	North Newbald, Galegate @	1963-1966	
97	Market Weighton, High Street @	1963-1967	@ 1963-1974
98	Withernsea Camp Shop	1963-1980	
	Bransholme Centre	1973-1982	1973-1982
	Mobile Grocery Shops	various	

General Grocery Warehouses:

Maple Street	1900-1909	
Hedon Road	1906-1909	
Osborne Street	1909-1941*	
Dansom Lane	1941-1955	
Canning Street	1955-1979	

Greenfruit only Branches:

Pocklington, Market Street	@	1956-1973
Willerby,141 Kingston Road		1957-1979

Greenfruit Warehouses:

Pier Street	1915-1923
Osborne Street	1923-1966
Dairycoates	1966-1972
Caroline Place	1972-1981

Wines and Spirits Branches:

4 Jameson Street	1967-1982
275 Anlaby Road	1967-1977
Beverley, 44 Toll Gavel	1967-1981

KEY: * destroyed by enemy action.
    @ date of transfer to Hull Society.
    $ converted to Krazy Kuts discount stores 1967/8.

By the late-1950s the Hull Co-op's multi-million pound Grocery business was conducted through nearly 90 branch shops scattered across East Yorkshire. There was a certain routine to branch life in which team spirit and co-operation, in every sense, were vital ingredients. This account, set mainly in the era before self-service shopping, has been compiled with the help of some of the people who experienced it at first hand:

Before the last war the majority of working class boys left school as soon as they reached 14. The position of Co-op Errand Boy was much coveted by those seeking a worthwhile career. Cyril Gardham, whose 47 years of Co-operative service took him from errand boy at Wellington Lane to chief clerk at Head Office, recalls how he came to be appointed: 'Lads leaving school would hear on the grapevine that the Co-op was setting on, and make their way down to the Grocery Warehouse in Osborne Street on a Saturday morning. Mr. Scarlett (the Shops Inspector) lined us all up and conducted the "interview" by walking up and down and casting an eye over us like a general inspecting his troops. If he liked what he saw, he would ask our name and where we lived, and tell us which shop to report to on Monday morning.'

'Please sir, I've come' was the way in which a shy beginner typically greeted his boss, on entering the world of work. His main duty was to deliver grocery orders to members' homes with either a handcart or carrier cycle. During the 1930s the rate for this job ranged from 10/6d. to 15/- a week - not bad pay in those days. Even the smallest of Co-op shops had enough regular work for a couple of handcart boys and a bicycle boy.

Goods made up into orders were packed into cartons which were stacked on the handcart in rows. To minimise repeat trips, boys would contrive to pile as many on as they could; 20 CWS Lard boxes was a good load. It is not always realised that a handcart was meant to be pulled rather than pushed; pushing was impracticable, at least on the outward run, because the boxes would obscure the way ahead. And in the winter a rope was often tied to the shafts

Charles Street Grocery in 1935. Note the coal prices listed, in shillings and pence, on the board (Picture by courtesy of Mr. J. Cottis, whose father Mr. Charles Cottis is third from left).

Horse-drawn Grocery van - a welcome sight on the North Hull housing estate in the 1930s. The driver announced its approach by shouting 'Grocers!' at the top of his voice every thirty seconds or so.

and passed across the boy's chest to give a firmer pull through the damp and slippery streets.

It was arduous work for a boy of 14, as Ron Jaques soon discovered on his first working day - New Year's Day 1938. Hull is noted for its flat terrain but it was Ron's misfortune to start at the Gillshill Road branch. His first deliveries, to the village of Sutton, involved a long slow drag up one of the few inclines in the area. He found the task getting harder and harder until eventually the cart ground to a complete halt and he just couldn't pull it any further. Noticing his plight, two elderly ladies rushed to the shop to tell the manager, Mr. Glen, who promptly despatched a 20-year-old counter hand to rescue him, leaving Ron's youthful ego in tatters!

Leslie Harling, who started work at De Grey Street in 1936 on 15/- a week, believes the Hull Co-op handcart was unique, as handcarts go, in having a metal rail running lengthways up and over the top: 'When it pelted down with rain we used to drape a green tarpaulin over the rail to protect the groceries. We looked just like little horses pulling tents along the road. But compared with Jackson's and Billy Cussons' lads, we felt like Kings, as they only had bikes! After our rounds, we raced our carts down the street to the Dairy Depot where they were garaged.'

Occasionally a handcart would come in useful for some other mission, such as the annual trek to the Guildhall to have the shop weights tested and stamped with the official validation mark. Or there was the time when young Maurice Ramsey broke his ankle while larking about, swinging from the rafters, at Sculcoates Lane. As no car could be found to convey him to Brook Street Casualty Department, he was unceremoniously trundled down Beverley Road on the back of the branch handcart!

The bike boy usually saw to the shorter deliveries, before dashing off to help his cart-pulling mates. But when Tony Rippon was set on at Strawberry Street in 1959 the handcarts were no more. Though slum clearance had decimated the catchment area of this tiny shop, the customers remained amazingly loyal, continuing to trade there long after moving out to the new estates miles away. Some reappeared every so often when visiting friends; others simply 'phoned their orders through. Like an intrepid explorer Tony would set forth on his bike, with an enormous cornflakes carton precariously perched over the front wheel, for the distant corners of Longhill or North Hull. Regular orders for huge sacks of washing soda also had to be taken to the local pubs. The bike's peculiar centre of gravity meant that if you braked too sharply or hit a bump it was liable to up-end without warning, depositing both rider and sacks in an undignified heap on the road. Ken Dearing, based at Cottingham Exeter Street, well remembers the experience: 'To get off the bike to deliver my first order I had to run alongside a wall or into a hedge. It was hair-raising at times.'

There were plenty of other tasks to fill an errand boy's working week. On arrival each morning he had to unhitch the wooden gates that protected the shop entrance overnight, and carry them through to the yard. Monday's cleaning routine involved washing the huge shop windows with a long-handled brush, brightening up all the glass display cases and polishing the weights on the scales with Brasso until they sparkled. And once a week he would mix sawdust and water to make a 'bran mash' and vigorously apply it to the wooden floors with a scrubbing brush.

Gordon Foster's induction to Co-op life, in 1934, was somewhat less conventional. He was put on the Society's first ever horse-drawn travelling shop, which served the North Hull housing estate. After drawing stock from Newland Avenue branch it plied a different round each day, Gordon's job being to assist the manager Mr. Richardson and driver Mr. Redhead: 'At weekends we were out till nine -

Chanterlands Avenue Grocery branch, 1922. The windows are crammed full of CWS products for an All-Co-operative Week sales drive. With its frontage barely altered, this building now houses a public library.

The stock room at Marfleet Grocery, showing the bins and chutes for flour, sugar and potatoes.

A successful Grocery branch depended on a happy staff with everyone doing their share. Team spirit seems in evidence in this 1960 snap taken at Bentley Grove (Picture by courtesy of Mrs B. Magee).

The finest flour for baking - CWS of course

all for no extra pay. The horse was young and at times a bit frisky; on the late shift the driver had to stand by its head to stop it galloping off. After the last customer was served we clambered aboard and the driver would pacify the animal and make a dash for the driving seat. Even with the handbrake fully on we put Ben Hur to shame and really shifted as the horse wanted to get home. At Newland Avenue the manager and I would jump off to put the cash in the safe and collect our bikes, and the horse would be away to the depot at full gallop with the brake still on.'

At the age of 16, youngsters who had proved themselves capable and trustworthy would be seeking an opening for a Warehouse Boy or Traveller. Those lucky enough to 'become superannuated' (i.e. make it on to the permanent staff) became the envy of their pals, for a job at the Co-op was regarded as a job for life, with pay rates and fringe benefits second to none. Our newly-apprenticed grocer was now expected to attend night school thrice weekly to master his trade. It was all rather reminiscent of school at first, with English, History and Arithmetic on the syllabus alongside Co-operative Book-keeping, Shop Practice and Commodities. As a salesman he would need a detailed knowledge of the articles sold - their countries of origin, production processes, grades, prices and so on - since customers often relied on his advice to make the correct choice and adopt the best storage and cooking methods. But the system was also designed to lay down firm foundations so that when he eventually became a Manager, with a branch of his own to look after, he had the confidence to run it properly.

The Warehouse Boy's duties included lifting and carrying, looking after the stock, putting together customers' orders and helping to unload deliveries. Flour, for example, was brought from the CWS Mill in ten stone sacks by a team of Shire horses. With home baking universally practised, housewives regularly ordered up to half a stone at a time and medium-sized branches like Princes Avenue went through 60

sacks a week. Bulky goods like flour, sugar and potatoes were winched up by the sackload to the stock rooms above the shop using an electrically-powered friction hoist, capable of handling loads of up to 5 cwt.

Long chutes fed down from an upstairs store room to the packing area, where a row of steel bins stood against one wall. There were separate bins for sugar, potatoes and the different grades of CWS flour - 4H (best white for baking); 3H and 2H (the cheaper grades for cooking and frying) - which the Warehouse Lad was expected to keep topped up. According to Cyril Gardham this apparently simple task was fraught with hazards for the raw recruit: 'If the shutter wasn't properly slammed down when you tipped flour down the chute, it would blow back in your face and cover you from head to toe. You crept downstairs looking like a snowman to face the boss's wrath. It wasn't your appearance that bothered him; he was thinking about his leakage result!' Cyril's Manager, Charlie Jones, summoned him to his office one day: 'What on earth have you been doing, Cyril,' he stormed, 'everyone's been getting brown bread.' 'But we don't sell any sir' came the puzzled reply. 'No, I know we don't lad. You must have tipped the brown flour down the white chute, you fool.' 'Mind you, the customers aren't complaining,' he added as an afterthought, 'they say it's the lightest brown bread they've ever baked!'

The Traveller's job was to call upon those members who were housebound or preferred to shop from home. He accepted payment for their previous order, sold them milk tokens and helped them complete their Weekly Order Book. After racing back to the store, 'putting up' the orders for the next day's deliveries could begin. For Co-op members it was the ultimate home-shopping service and all at no extra charge. With a week's grace before settling up, the food was often consumed before it had been paid for.

Some branches had several big country rounds.

Ken Dearing regularly collected in 60 order books each from Skidby, Dunswell and Woodmansey, for later delivery by motor van. Alf Brough of Bridlington High Street preferred his own racing cycle to the clumsy standard-issue bike for his weekly trips to West Huntow, Boynton, Bempton, Carnaby, Thornholme and Wilsthorpe. For him the job had mixed blessings: 'Everyone thought how lucky you were to have an outdoor job, but it could be pretty rough during the long winter months.' An enterprising Traveller used his initiative to sell a few special lines on his rounds. John Kirby - who made his 200-mile weekly trips from Withernsea branch by van - was rewarded with VIP treatment at the Crumpsall Biscuit Works after selling 2,000 packets of CWS biscuits during a four-week campaign in 1962. His counterpart at Cottingham, Keith Kirk, managed to shift six CWS one-bar electric fires for 27/- each in just three days.

Promotion to the rank of Junior Assistant brought our aspiring young grocer into the sales area proper. But the chance to hone his selling skills was still fairly limited. During the early part of the week, when trade was relatively slack, his help would be needed to prepare for sale the many commodities that, years ago, every shop had to break down from bulk.

Dorothy Moore spent an entire summer weighing and wrapping in the stock-room at Bridlington Chapel Street to meet the demands of the town's holidaymakers and seaside landladies: 'We had to handle each commodity in a logical sequence to avoid cross-contamination. Flour was packed into white bags containing ¼, ½ or 1 stone. Dried fruit from 56lb. blocks had to be scooped on to different coloured paper squares, according to type, and then flat-wrapped - a folding and tucking technique that took some mastering at first. Yeast, cereals and sweets were placed in paper cups that you spun by hand.' There was quite a knack to securing the funnel-shaped packs so they didn't come undone. And packing soap flakes into 1lb. bags often induced a bout of sneezing - just the job to clear a stuffed up nose.

Sixteen stone sacks of sugar were emptied into a metal bath. A team of three - one filling the stiff blue bags, another weighing, and a third wrapping - packed it in denominations of ½, 1, 2, 3, 4 and 6lbs. A practised filler could judge the amount to within a few grains but for the person wrapping the test of success was to drop the packet on the floor to see if it stayed closed. The trio beavered away until all the sugar was neatly stacked in the shop fixtures. Only if the Leading Assistant called them away to deal with a queue of customers was their rhythm disturbed.

Most Hull Co-op branches followed a stereotyped pattern, with 'dry' groceries at one side; provisions at the other. The packing area was along the back wall while, in a two-door shop, the confectionery counter occupied the space between the doors. Each shop had a remarkably similar layout so that staff transferring from one to another could easily locate the stock. The Confectionery section was usually run by a woman or girl. At close of business any unsold stock had to be placed in special cool drawers beneath the counter. The errand boys at some branches used to think it the height of wit to tease the poor pastry girl about her 'lead-lined drawers'.

For years it was Society policy not to employ women who had a husband to support them. To prevent favouritism the employment of close relatives was also frowned upon. Former Confectionery Assistant Barbara Kitching's experience was probably fairly common: 'My husband-to-be worked at the same branch and we had to keep it dark when we started seeing each other because you weren't supposed to go out with anyone from work. After our engagement I had to leave my ring at home. Of course, when we got married I was forced to leave, and my sister stepped into my job the next day.' Dorothy Coates of Beverley believes she was the first woman to be kept on after marriage: 'It was 1940 and, with the men away at war, they were in a real fix. A special Committee meeting was held one Saturday afternoon to decide that I could stay.'

The Provisions section generally warranted a Senior and a Junior Provisions Hand. Boning and rolling the sides of bacon that arrived in hessian sacks from the CWS (Dansom Lane) was a highly-skilled operation. Often a piano wire was used to take the meat cleanly off the bone. As the sides were all 'charged in' at one price, there was quite an art to working out how to get your money back by pricing the choice cuts and the less popular ones suitably. A good bacon man was worth his weight in gold. Little wonder that many felt held back in their career; once allowed to rise to First Hand their valuable skills were lost to that branch.

Before refrigeration came in, money could soon be lost on provisions. Apart from CWS Red Seal and Silver Seal margarine, which were pre-packed, everything had to be made up in the store. Casks of Danish butter and wooden crates containing New Zealand butter or CWS lard were tipped out on to the marble counter and divided up into packs graded from 2oz. to 1lb. But in high summer they were brought out only on demand, or the packs would melt before the assistant's eyes. Tins of corned beef (for which most Co-ops had a ready sale at 2½d. a quarter or 9d. a lb.) had to be steeped in buckets of cold water, otherwise the meat became impossible to slice.

During the Society's expansionary years new branches were continually coming on stream; promotion prospects for those willing to work hard were rosy. A large branch employed several grades of Assistant and so it wasn't long before a keen counter hand had a chance to prove himself by 'acting up' for a colleague on holiday or sick leave. Those aspiring to First Hand would pester their boss for permission to take a Co-op Union correspondence course and

sit the necessary exams. The redoubtable Mr. Scarlett, whose job it was to assess the Society's needs, would carefully scrutinise the list of passes.

The First Hand was responsible for overseeing the cashing up and banking of takings. The larger branches originally had a glass-fronted cash booth in the centre, connected to each serving point by overhead cash railway. It fell to the errand boy to climb up and grease the wires of this contraption every Monday morning. And if there was an attractive young lady cashier, the assistants found a novel use for it when the boss wasn't around. Cryptic notes containing invitations to the Pictures and other sundry propositions winged their way across the ceiling as did, no doubt, the subsequent messages of rejection!

In the 1920s all branches were equipped with safes and wooden Gledhill Tills costing £80 apiece. Shop cashiers were dispensed with and each assistant was made responsible for his own till and cash box. The check system served a dual purpose: to calculate members' purchases and act as a control on the employee's honesty, since every check given had to be matched by equivalent cash. Any 'overs' and 'shorts' had to be explained to the satisfaction of Head Office or the assistant risked having a black mark on their service record.

One often hears it said that customer service at the Co-op was painfully slow compared with other grocers. On busy Friday and Saturday mornings it was nothing unusual to have to stand in a queue for 20 minutes. Philip Meldrum's mother, who shopped at Brindley Street, used to say: 'No wonder their motto is *Labor and Wait* - they labour while you wait!' The problem wasn't the fault of the hard-working staff; it was all the extra duties required of them. While their private trade counterparts could devote their full attention to selling, Co-op personnel also had to issue milk tokens, take coal orders, book boot repairs in and out, deal with Penny Banks, sell savings stamps, handle members' check sheets *and* take Ballot Club payments for the Drapery Department. Unless the volume of business warranted a separate desk, all these transactions took place at the Grocery counter, distracting staff from the main task of selling food.

Check sheets were a particular chore: 'Members were supposed to change them for a red check as soon as they were full but many used to save them up and present them in great batches, with the checks stuck on all higgledy-piggledy. They were a real nightmare to reckon up,' one former Assistant recalls.

Joyce Cook has vivid memories of accompanying her mother on shopping trips to Londesborough Street Co-op: 'It fascinated me to hear the assistants call out, at intervals (and they had to shout really loud to make themselves heard through in the warehouse) - "Quarter stone of Best!" "Quarter stone of spuds!" and so on. Presently a little boy in a white coat, and an apron so long that I wondered how he managed not to trip over it, would appear from the back with the order.' If you wanted anything from the provisions counter you were given a little ticket to take across to the other side of the shop, only to endure another wearying wait. Children became adept at inventing any excuse to avoid being sent on errands to the Co-op, for they were invariably kept waiting until the adults had all been served. Whether this signifies a greater deference to seniority than exists today, or the staff simply failed to notice them over the wide counters, is a moot point with the older generation.

Something that made a deep and lasting impression on one employee in the 1930s was the grinding poverty endured by many Co-op customers: 'Children regularly came in after school asking for three or sixpenn'orth of bacon bits, which we kept in a box under the counter. With a deftness of hand that would have impressed Paul Daniels we used to whip a full

slice off the counter and drop it on the paper - that was for Dad or Mum's tea. Some customers only had five or six items listed in their order books - chiefly flour, sugar and fats; that was their entire week's grocery order. And one poor woman paid 3d. a week at the back of her book for a Christmas treat - a rabbit.'

How people lived a hand to mouth existence is illustrated by this tale from Doug Widdowson who, as errand boy at Franklin Street, delivered to the terraces off Holderness Road. In this close-knit community, when the offspring of a big family married, they often set up home close to their parents. The mother would bring in an order for each of her married daughters and perhaps one or two neighbours as well: 'She presented us with a big sheet of paper headed "Lily", "Mary", "Blanche" etc. listing all their various wants. We added it up; Mother owed us, and they in turn owed her. Workmen were paid Saturday lunch time and usually called at the pub on the way home to break into their wages. Often the Co-op errand lad would be waiting impatiently to take round a cartload of food when they finally rolled home. You see, the Society had a rule that we couldn't leave any goods until the previous week's order was paid for. The poor woman of the house couldn't settle up till her old man arrived with his pay packet. So Lily, Mary and Blanche were all there standing on their doorsteps waiting for their orders!'

Stories abound of how the Co-op helped the very poor: 'Families were given half-crown or five-bob food tickets by the Parish Guardians, made out for the basic essentials of life. Shopkeepers weren't supposed to exchange them for anything else, but we would often slip in a few biscuits or a tin of peaches and get away with it,' Alf Brough admitted. 'After all, we were a Co-operative Society and we knew our social history.' One lady remembers the Co-op as the only shop that would let her husband have ½oz. of Old Friend Tobacco or five Woodbines 'on the Parish'. Being a docker, he was often without

HULL CO-OPERATIVE SOCIETY LIMITED

GROCERY ORDER BOOK.

Member's Name ....

Address...

....

Share No.................. Ledger Folio.................

Branch ....

IMPORTANT NOTICE.

CHECK SHEETS should be handed in for Final Receipt the FIRST WEEK in March and September.

N.D. CHECKS issued in respect of proprietary goods must be affixed to a green non-dividend bearing Check Sheet.

PASS BOOKS should be forwarded to Jarratt Street Office the LAST WEEK in March and September.

Country Members to hand their books to the Grocery Branch.

JARRATT STREET OFFICE HOURS:

10 a.m. to 1 p.m. & 2-30 to 4 p.m. except Thursday, close 12 noon. Saturday open until 5 p.m.

REMINDER LIST.

Description of Goods	Description of Goods	Description of Goods
Almonds, Whole	Firewood	Oil, Camphorated
„ Ground	Force Fresh Fish	„ Castor
Arrowroot, Ground	Flour	„ Cod Liver
Aerated Waters	„ Self-raising	„ and Malt Ex.
Ammonia	Floor Polish	Paint
All-in-One	Fruit—Green	Peas. Peas, Split
Bread Bacon	Ginger, Root	Peels Pepper
Boots (Repairs)	„ Ground	Parrot Foods
Butter	Glycerine	Pea Flour
Barley, Pearl	Gravy Browning	Pickling Spice
„ Patent	„ Salt	Plum Puddings
Blue	Grits, Oyster Shell	Pickles (all kinds)
Bird Seed, Bird Sand	„ Flint	Potatoes
Boot Polishes	Grape Nuts	Raisins
Black Lead	Groats	Rice
Butter Beans	Health Salts	Sugar
Baking Powder	Honey	Sultanas
Borax Bovril.	Handles, Broom	Salt
Beans, Baked	Jellies, Jelly Crystals	Syrup, Golden
Blanc Mange Powders	Jams (all kinds)	Sutox
Bun Flour	Kellogs' Corn Flakes	Seidlitz Powder.
Bath Brick Powder	Lemon Curd	Seeds, Caraway
Biscuits (all kinds)	Liquorice Powder	Saltpetre
Carb. Soda	Lentils	Semolina
Canned Goods	Lemonade Crystals	Soda Starch
Cherries, Glace	Linseed, Whole	Sandwich Powders
Chest and Lung Mxt.	„ Ground	Shortex
Cloves	Liquid Metal Polish	Soaps, Washing
Coals	Lactic Cheese	„ Toilet
Cream of Tartar	Lard, Refined	„ Dry
Custard Powders	Milk, Condensed	Sauces
Chocolates	„ Evaporated	Tapioca
Cornflour	Matches, Paraffin	Tartaric Acid
Cheese	„ Swan Vestas	Tea
Cocoa	Margarine	Toilet Paraffin
Coffee	Marmalade	Turpentine
Candles	Medicines, Patent	Toilet Rolls
Cream Tints	Medicinal Paraffin	Tobaccos
Currants	Malted Milk	Vegetables
Candied Peel	Mustard	Vinegar
Desiccated Cokernut	Macaroni Nutmegs	Vermicelli
Dried Fruits	Nuts (all kinds)	Varnish Stains
Dog Biscuits	Night Lights	Virol, Virol and Milk
Egg Powders	Oats, Cremo	Whiting
Emery Paper	Oatmeal	Wines, Fruit
Eggs, English	Oxo Cubes. Oxo	Water Glass
„ Pickled	Oil, Olive	Yeast

FRESH FISH DELIVERED WEDNESDAYS AND FRIDAYS

The Society provided members with a ruled note book in which to jot down their weekly requirements. The 1944 version had a handy reminder list at the back (By courtesy of Mrs M. Groves).

Typical pre-war Grocery branch interior. Note how neatly the tins and packets fit into the wall fixtures, also the elaborate counter fronts, all hand-moulded by the Society's joiners.

Mr. Reg Lamb serving at the Provisions counter, Greenwood Avenue, 1960. In a highly competitive business, skill in handling Provisions was important for building up regular custom (Picture by courtesy of Mr. R. Lamb).

CWS Tea and Coffee display, Arcade branch. Branch managers often developed a special flair for window dressing and took great pride in creating imaginative displays, sometimes in their own time. Themed competitions were organised, with prizes donated by the suppliers.

work for weeks on end and the family had no money coming in at all. The Co-op was a real friend at these times. To help them get by, Branch Managers would allow trusted members to 'draw down' their £2 share capital in groceries. Finding herself with an empty coal house on returning to Hull after evacuation, the same lady popped round to the Co-op in Endymion Street: 'Don't worry love, by the time you get home, there'll be a bag of coal waiting for you,' the assistant promised. And sure enough there was. It was this willingness to go that bit further to help the least fortunate members of the community that made the Co-op stand out as an institution among shops.

This concept of social service manifested itself in the strangest of ways. When, in 1973, the Directors announced the closure of the Bentley Grove branch, at the heart of a Hull Corporation housing estate, the Society received several letters of protest from residents. The tenor of this correspondence was not so much the loss of the grocery service, but how they were going to miss their daily conversations with the cheery staff. For the lonely and isolated the loss of their Co-op store could be like the demise of a much-loved companion.

The smooth running of the store was entrusted to the Branch Manager, whose daily duties broadly included ordering the stock, managing the staff, attending to all the paperwork and dressing the shop windows. He was also answerable to 'top management' for producing a profit each half-year. But to his staff he was often seen as a kind of father-figure; indeed, one well-known character at Bridlington rejoiced in the nickname 'Pop' Wright. Smartly dressed in a short black jacket and pin-striped trousers, the archetypal Co-op Manager was a pillar of his East Riding community; a respected figure to whom people turned for advice. He was just as content to witness a customer's Will as to pack their grocery order. Not for nothing were certain esteemed holders of the position dubbed 'The Mayor of Hornsea' or 'The Mayor of Howden'

by their city cousins. They may not actually have worn civic regalia but what they didn't know about their respective townships probably wasn't worth knowing.

The country branches dabbled in 'Drapery', a term embracing everything from shirts, jackets and boots to dolly tubs, tin baths, linoleum, paraffin and pots and pans. It was run on the principle 'if we haven't got it, we'll get it for you'. Significant business was also done with the farmers in offals or animal feeds. Bran and Sharps from the CWS Flour Mill and Wheat, Barley and Maize were supplied in huge sacks. Cyril Harrison remembers a barter system operating at Newport, the farmers keeping the shop stocked with butter and eggs in part-payment for their grocery order. Contrary to popular belief, country folk were some of the Society's staunchest supporters, 100% membership being quite common among the farming fraternity. Members were found in the tiniest hamlets, miles from the nearest Co-op store. Leslie Harling's aunt lived 'out in the sticks' near Leconfield: 'She was a real Co-op-ite and wouldn't have bought her food or coal anywhere else. The Traveller called for her order every week as regularly as clockwork.'

One of the manager's duties was keeping the debt ledger. A large branch might have £1,000 worth of small debts outstanding at any one time, all meticulously recorded in thick ledgers. Members were only allowed a week's credit but some inevitably got into difficulties and said, 'I'll square up once I get my Divi.' When the Office returned the updated share book, the manager had to be quick to intercept it before the member came in! At half-year end a lot of midnight oil was burned at home balancing up the ledgers and making out a list of names and amounts owing for the Credit Department. Before long they would come on the 'phone: 'On page 280, I see you have a large debt outstanding; what do you propose to do about it?' It was a constant source of anxiety.

Another twice-yearly chore was stocktaking, which was done after closing time or on a Sunday. A member of the Management Committee was assigned to each shop as Stockchecker. Shortly afterwards the manager received a brown envelope ominously marked 'Private and Confidential'. It contained his Leakage Statement, prepared by Cyril Wingfield at Head Office, revealing the shop's results. Leakage control was a means of assessing whether the inflow of cash matched the throughput of stock. There were many reasons why this might not be so, such as poor stock control, shrinkage, pilfering and bad debts. Any manager whose results fell outside certain limits was summonsed before the General Grocery Manager. According to one: 'Results were everything. Persistently bad leakages meant we were destined for a smaller shop to make way for some promising young First Hand. There's always someone ready to step into your shoes, they used to say.' Conversely, the consistent star performers might be offered a better shop. To be promoted to one of the 'posher' suburban branches was considered the acme of achievement for a Hull Co-op grocer.

There were certain people whose arrival in the branch was always guaranteed to have the manager and staff on their toes. People like the Shops Inspector, whose job it was to keep a sharp eye on the standards of shopkeeping. Their visits were supposed to be unannounced, but the Hull Co-op's well-developed bush telegraph usually afforded some advance warning! Then there were the Co-op Guildswomen. Having a big say in the way the Society was run, they were widely regarded as demi-gods: 'When a Guildswoman entered the shop the staff nearly stood to attention. We took great care over serving them; anything amiss and we were bound to hear about it later.' The Management Committee had the authority to visit the branches too. 'We were scared stiff of them as well! One or two of them allowed the power to go to their head a bit and went round finding fault with nearly everything in sight.'

Physical conditions in the shops often left a lot to be desired. Most branches lacked any form of heating and so, for the counter staff, winter was synonymous with chilblains. But in at least one worker's opinion the homely atmosphere more than compensated for the chilly environment: 'There was a great sense of togetherness that saw you through good times and bad. Colleagues would take care of one another when they suffered troubles. This feeling extended to the customers too, and you made a habit of asking after the family's health just as if they were an extension of your own.' Such sentiments are echoed time after time when recounting experience of Co-operative employment: 'The work was hard and the routine strict but it was a marvelllous organisation to work for; a real community in fact.'

But nothing stays the same for ever. In the late-1950s the winds of change began to whistle through the Department as more shops changed over to self-service. Products started to arrive in store ready packed, with attractive labels designed to sell themselves without the intervention of a knowledgeable time-served grocer. It stripped a large part of the skill, and a lot of the enjoyment, out of the job. Many long-serving, dyed in the wool Co-op grocers became disgruntled with the new regime and departed for other jobs, some making a complete career change midway through their working lives. Becoming a Co-op Insurance agent was a popular move - for some it meant staying in touch with the same familiar circle of customers - while others went into local government or the Civil Service.

Faced with competition from the new cut-price stores, the Society was forced to review some of its time-honoured practices. A costing exercise in 1966 showed that those branches still employing a Traveller were losing at least 2/- on every order collected from a member's home.

Branch Managers' Association visits to the CWS Tobacco Factory, Sharp Street, Manchester, were always popular. On the 1947 'trip' we can identify:
Back row: Messrs. Atkinson, Cox, Woodcock, Andrews, Coggin, Milner, Symons, Booth, Owst, West, Credland, Storey, Staveley, Conner, Booth, Bowden, Haines.
Middle: Clark J., Stephenson, Clark G., Norton, Pricket, Walker, Dent, Bowden, Cawley, Hoose, Jackson, Brent, Widdowson, Stephenson, Carr, Sumpton, Baxter, -, Wilson, Fleetwood, Watson, -, Needler, Gibson, -, Mann, Glen, -, Foster.
Seated: Woolans, Langfield, Carr, CWS rep., Ledger, Stone, Peddie, Kirk, Thirsk, Downs, -, Everett, Anderson. (Picture by courtesy of Mr. Doug Widdowson).

The oddly-named Green Fruit Section at 440 Anlaby Road.

The loss was greater still by the time the one million orders a year had actually been delivered. The time had come to phase in Cash & Carry trading. Some shops were completely stripped out and wooden fixtures, cheaply knocked together by the Society's joiners, were installed and piled high with basic lines at knock-down prices. With a jazzy new name (Krazy Kuts) over the door, the customers came pouring in.

But progress with self-service conversion was rather long drawn out. In a report to the Board in 1970 the newly-appointed Grocery Manager, Bill Devonald, observed that 29 shops were still operating on counter-service principles. He recommended an accelerated programme of either modernisation or closure. By the time the last example, at Patrington, was phased out in 1976, the supermarket had become an established feature of most towns - and the age of the giant superstore had already dawned.

In the couple of decades since, retail technology has advanced by leaps and bounds; consumer demand and shopping habits have altered beyond recognition. The operation of a present-day Co-operative food store now bears little resemblance to that described above. Will the wheel turn full circle to allow Co-op members to do all their shopping once again from the comfort of their home? If it does, it will most likely involve the use of computer terminal rather than the simple Weekly Order Book so fondly remembered by countless Hull and East Riding folk. Only time will tell.

BUTCHERY DEPARTMENT

Managers:

T. Best
A. Fox
P. Davies
G. Ball
T.W. Taylorson
A.W. Cuthbertson

Slaughterhouse and Pork Factory:

44 Pelham Street	1915-1935
9 Hessle Road	1928-1935
Commerce Lane (Cattle Lairage)	1932-1941
Great Thornton Street	1935-1968
Caroline Place	1968-1981

Branches: (as listed under Grocery plus the following specialist shops)

44 Pelham Street	1915-1960	
229 Beverley Road	1915-1966	
Market Place	1921-1928	
3-7 Hessle Road	1928-1963	
Howden	1930-1935	
300 Marfleet Lane	1938-1986	
328 Southcoates Lane	1939-1968	1974-1981
Willerby, 139 Kingston Road	1939-1981	
571 Holderness Road	1945-1969	
446 Anlaby Road	1949-1974	
Howden, 25 Bridgegate	1954-1973	
414 Staveley Road	1954-1973	
197 Portobello Street	1954-1976	
6 Hantom Grove	1955-1963	
Pocklington, Clarke's Lane	*1956-1958	
771 Hessle Road	1957-1966	
Ings Road Centre	1967-1983	
Bransholme, 2 Yatesbury Garth	1971-1975	
Mobile Butchery Shops	various	

* date of transfer to Hull Society

The Management Committee were initially cautious about Butchery; it had so many pitfalls. Processing carcasses was at best an unpredictable business and its narrow profit margins meant that other departments generally had to subsidise its contribution to the dividend.

In 1915 the Society finally decided to take the plunge and bought out Mr. Frederick Roll's Slaughterhouse and Porkery business in

Mobile Butchery fleet lined up for a publicity cavalcade in 1936. The Hull Co-op obtained good service from its vehicles - some of these Morris vans were still traversing the highways and by-ways of East Yorkshire in the 1960s.

'Service with a smile' at the fresh meat counter in the Skyline Pantry.

Drypool. The first shops sold only pork and were referred to as Pork branches; beef, mutton and poultry were added later when wartime restrictions came off. Expansion came gradually, chiefly in parallel with the Grocery business. The usual practice of placing separately-managed Grocery and Butchery shops adjacent to each other enabled customers simply to walk from one door to the next to do all their food shopping.

An important business acquisition was that of Mr. Herbert Porter, a well-known Hessle Road butcher who bought at Smithfield, when he retired in July 1928. The deal included premises known as Randerson's Buildings with three small shops and an abattoir. A plot at the rear was developed as a cattle lairage where beasts arriving from market could be rested prior to slaughter.

A paragraph in the Society's Report for June 1930 suggests that Co-op members were as concerned about animal welfare then as they are today: 'It will no doubt be of interest to all members that the Society has taken a lead in humane slaughtering of animals, for it now employs the most painless methods science has devised and which are approved by many leading authorities.'

The Slaughterhouse and Pork Factory in Great Thornton Street - opened on 10th October 1935 - were the operational headquarters for 33 years until a Compulsory Purchase Order forced their relocation to Caroline Place. The Pork Factory turned out all the Society's requirements for sausages, boiled and pressed hams, tongues, black-puddings, polonies, saveloys, tripe, potted meat, haslet, brawn and so on.

According to Stan Clixby, the typical small shop was virtually a 'one man band' with the butcher responsible for everything from butchering to window dressing, stock control, scrubbing down, cash and book-keeping and of course turning in a profit at the end of the day. A state

of rivalry, friendly or otherwise, sometimes existed between managers of adjoining Grocery and Butchery shops. There was plenty to be at loggerheads over, such as the use of each other's fridges, allowing sawdust sweepings to litter the yard and the way Head Office apportioned the property costs. Each manager would be firmly convinced he was bearing some of the other's charges, a matter of no small consequence when his pay was based on results!

Usually an errand lad was taken on to make home deliveries. Becoming a butcher's boy on leaving school at 14 was the traditional route of entry into this worthwhile craft occupation. Courses for apprentices were run at the Osborne Street Centre but most of the required know-how was picked up simply by watching the butcher at work.

In the country districts it was necessary to reverse the usual order of things and take the shop to its customers. By 1936 the Co-op had five travelling shops, plying their rounds at set weekly times to serve the East Riding's villages and farmsteads. The Beverley round spanned a wide arc from Walkington across to Leconfield and Leven while the Howden van visited South Cave, Newport and Saltmarshe. The Hessle van called at North Ferriby, Elloughton and Brough. And there were two Holderness rounds, one extending to Sproatley; the other penetrating as far as Sunk Island and the Lifeboat Station at Spurn Point.

Bob Crowe - 'Butcher Bob' as he was known - spent 40 years on the road: 'It was a grand life. We got to know all our customers and their families well; many of them became firm friends. The only problem was when we had to collect debts. If a member failed to pay up promptly we had to send the Office a card to get permission to stop the owings out of their next Divi. As you can imagine, on the next visit our name was Mudd!' '

'Monday was settling-up day when no rounds

were worked. We spent the day at base writing up our time-sheets, ordering stationery, cashing up and handing over the previous week's takings, which we had kept on our person over the week-end. The possibility of being robbed never entered our head. It was the same when visiting lonely farms; if my assistant was away I thought nothing about leaving the van unattended down the lane.'

The last war was a turbulent time for the meat trade. All slaughterhouses came under the direction of the Ministry of Food. The Co-op - which now operated slaughterhouses in Blanket Row and Sewer Lane besides Great Thornton Street - became responsible for processing and distributing most of the English meat supplies of a large district extending as far as Bridlington. A lot of contract business was also picked up from the wartime canteens that were set up around the city.

When meat rationing ended in July 1954, the way was clear for expansion and the Department quickly attained its maximum size of 60 shops. But the 1960s brought fresh challenges as population drift left many older branches high and dry, their takings often insufficient even to pay the butcher's wages. Shopping habits and economics now favoured the comprehensive food hall, offering the shopper's complete needs under one roof. A mass closure programme was therefore set in motion and pre-packed meat - prepared at the Pork Factory and sold through the Grocery - was introduced at some locations. But with its output restricted to Co-op shops the Pork Factory was denied the economies of scale now needed for profitable operation. Following the merger with CRS in 1981 it too was closed and supplies were taken from specialist firms.

Today's supermarkets offer a choice of meat and allied products that would have amazed the Co-op butcher of yesteryear. The meat is all obtained from quality-assured sources and hygienically packed before arriving at the store, where the closest attention possible is paid to temperature control, display and labelling.

BAKERY DEPARTMENT

Managers:

T. Yates
- Armitage
- Tunnard
E. Webster
G.L. Mackman
V. Bourne
T. Seffen
F. Johnson
A.L. Niccols
E. Wilson

Bakeries:

Caroline Place	1906-1971
Howden	1916-1931
Bridlington Marshall Ave.	1916-1924
Bridlington West Street	1924-1930

The Society acquired Messrs. Little's bakehouse in Caroline Place, Hull in 1906, extending it several times as the business grew. There were three operational floors: The Bread Bakery and Despatch on the ground floor, Confectionery and Cake Decorating on the first, and the ingredients store on the second.

According to long-serving worker Len Pounder, it used to take three 16-man shifts to produce the Society's daily bread requirements. Flour, yeast, lard and water were mixed together to make a 40 stone bowl of dough, which was left to prove (rise) for up to four hours. It was chopped up, moulded on tables and dropped into a mechanical dough-divider which dispensed even sized pieces for either one- or two-pound loaves. Next it was loaded into tins which had been greased with a mop-stick dipped in whale oil and left to prove again before transfer to the ovens. All these stages demanded some form of manual intervention.

There were six massive coke-fired ovens, each with two large drawplates capable of baking 200 loaves at a time. Crusty Vienna loaves and pork pies were baked in a peel oven, for which a peel (a long flat spade) was used to load the iron trays; there was quite an art to fishing them out quickly enough to prevent the back trays burning. 'Taking off' the ovens kept six men busy and each time they were opened up the entire district was treated to the wonderful aroma of freshly-baked bread.

Charlie Limon was an Oven Man in the 1930s. His daughter Jean remembers him setting off for work in the early hours: 'Father was in charge of stoking and filling the ovens. It was such hot work that by the end of the shift his overalls would be wringing with sweat. He was a keen Union man and liked looking after his gang. They would take bacon and sausages in for him to cook for their breakfast in a tin plate in one of the ovens; for his trouble they rewarded him with cigarettes.'

Until 1930 all bread was sold loose. The first primitive wrapping equipment still needed an operator to fold the waxed paper around each loaf individually. But with this innovation the demand for Co-op Bread increased considerably.

On the Confectionery floor, pastry was made on large sandstone tables and repeatedly fed through huge rollers which were gradually tightened up until the desired thickness was attained. It was then knocked-out with a tin ring and placed in moulded trays to be filled with lemon curd, ground rice or custard. On the same floor Miss Florrie Coggin supervised a team of girls icing buns and hand-decorating Anniversary Cakes. Toffee, sweets and Easter Eggs were manufactured at one time on the floor above.

Until road transport improved, local bakeries at Howden and Bridlington ensured fresh supplies for those outposts and minimised breakages in transit. Arthur Moore, of the Bridlington Grocery staff, recalled pastries arriving at his shop in a 'frightful box-like affair, with two wheels at the front and one behind. It was powered by a motorbike engine and we called the lad driving it Buck Jones because, perched up over the rear wheel, he looked as if he was riding a horse'.

The Board appointed a Bakery Sub-Committee whose enviable duty it was to sample the products. With eyes firmly fixed on the opposition, they would send round to Wm. Jackson's for a loaf in order to compare the weight, quality and price. A 1914 Minute stipulated: 'Hot X Buns to be no less size than Jackson's and sold at same price - 9d. a dozen.' Another time Battenburg and Hindenburg cakes were exhibited for the Committee which, after due deliberation, declared itself satisfied 'that ours are better than anybody else's Burgs'.

In the run up to Christmas the staff worked all hours to meet the demand for pork pies, all moulded by hand and filled with meat from the Pork Factory. 'They used to say there wasn't a pork pie in Yorkshire to beat the Hull Co-op's,' one former worker claims. And at Hull Fair time it was all hands on deck to turn out huge quantities of Brandy Snap. The staff could take home any damaged items but Len Pounder used to turn unsold stock into Ginger Cookies - very popular when other 'goodies' were on ration. Saturday lunch time was clear-out time when people queued at the door for a sixpenny bagful of stale buns or cheesecakes. Even the flour dust from sacks and floor sweepings was turned into Pig Bread for sale to local farmers.

In its heyday the Bakery employed 200 workers. It had a lively social life what with canteen sing-songs and grand Departmental Dances at Beverley Road Baths. Jean Frisby (nee Limon) takes up her story: 'When I was 14 it was taken for granted I would join Father at the Bakery. My first job was to mark chocolate circles on Maids with a knife. It was hard to keep up and I used to plead with Father not to bake any more. He would say, "I've got no choice love" but then come over and lend a hand.'

After six months the Manager, Mr. Frank Johnson, promoted her to Telephonist, under Miss Minnie Payne. 'There were four of us and we started ringing round the branch shops at nine, carefully noting down their confectionery orders on pads. We soon got to know all the 'phone numbers by heart and the pastry girls used to say they could set their clocks by us. The total for each line was chalked up on a big board so the bakers knew how much to produce for the next morning's deliveries.'

The Bakery gobbled up Society capital as it strove to keep pace with the constant progress in baking technology. The biggest change of all came on 6th March 1950 when the old drawplate ovens were finally taken out of service. In their place was a Baker Perkins 9-sack Uniflow automatic bread plant, which could turn out 2,000 loaves an hour, three times as many as before. Together with high-speed dough mixers, conveyor belts and new bread slicers, it reduced staffing needs by at least half. Manual labour was still needed to de-pan the loaves but no more than eight operatives per shift. Whether Co-op Bread - once widely acclaimed as 'the best loaf in Hull' - ever tasted quite the same again was, however, a moot point.

The extra capacity meant the Bakery could bid for contract work. By 1953 it was supplying all the daily needs of the York, Goole, Market Weighton, Pocklington, Malton & Norton and Scarborough Co-operative Societies. But by the late-1960s the tide had turned. Faced with a changing market, shrinking shop network and ageing plant, Management decided to cease large loaf production altogether and take a daily supply from the CWS at Leeds. The vacated space was converted into a Pork Factory.

The standard of confectionery baking still took

some beating however. In 1967 the Hull Co-op took five prizes in a National Baking Contest at Newcastle. Production Manager Mr. E. Wilson took two Firsts and a Challenge Cup; Foreman Mr. A. Todd gained a Second, and the Apprentice Cup went to John Morris.

By 1971 rumours were circulating among the 71 staff and two Unions that the Bakery was under threat of closure. Management eventually called everyone to a meeting in the Co-op Institute to hear their fate. The Directors issued a statement: 'Over the last two years the economics of our own production have been considered by the Board. As more shops were converted to self-service loose confectionery was not having the sales expected. More public demand was for boxed confectionery. There were also problems relating to the cost of delivery to the many branch shops in Hull and outside. The Directors decided to seek offers for the supply of bread and confectionery direct to shops and have approached various suppliers. The Board took the decision with the greatest reluctance and, being anxious to look after the welfare of the staff, interviews are being arranged with other bakers.'

It was a sad blow for the workers, many of whom had spent a lifetime at the Bakery. Production ceased on 16th June 1971, bringing down the curtain on 65 years of Co-operative Baking in Hull. With the ultimate touch of irony, long-time rivals Wm. Jackson & Son Ltd. won the contract to supply the Society's shops.

DAIRY DEPARTMENT

Managers:

J. McManus
W.A. Stansfield
D.E. Ralph NDA NDD

Processing Dairy: Great Thornton Street, Hull   1915-1968

In the early years of the Bakery hand vans brought fresh bread and pastries to the doors of members in East and West Hull.

Bread Bakery in Caroline Place, 1907. In those days all the loaves were transported to the shops in huge wicker baskets and sold unwrapped.

Charlie Limon (second from left) and gang removing finished loaves from the ovens. Each oven had two sliding drawplates, the upper one resting on folding legs. The plates were changed in turn to give a total baking time of up to 50 minutes for a large loaf. The timer clocks are visible over the oven doors.

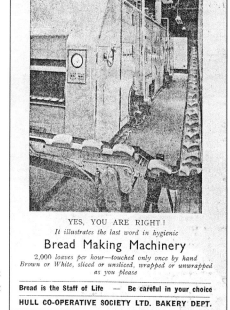

Automatic bread plant 1950-67. The loaves twisted and turned, in roller-coaster fashion, through the oven before emerging on to a moving belt to be conveyed to the cooling room.

Distribution Depots: De La Pole Avenue; Clumber Street; De Grey Street; Cleveland Street; Holland Street; Marfleet; Stoneferry Road; Boothferry Road; Anlaby Common; First Avenue; County Road; Westminster Avenue; Greenwich Avenue; Hessle, Northfield; Beverley; Withernsea; Hornsea; Howden; Bridlington, West Street.

For more than fifty years the Hull Co-operative Society was a principal supplier of milk to families and schoolchildren in East Yorkshire. The original premises in Great Thornton Street were quickly outgrown and so some adjoining cottages were bought and redeveloped by the Society's own Works Department. The greatly enlarged and modernised premises were opened by Dr. Nicolas Gebbie (Hull's Medical Officer of Health) on 16th June 1932.

A souvenir brochure issued for the occasion described the production process: Milk arriving from the farms each morning was first of all sampled and tested in the laboratory. It was then tipped into a portable hopper and pumped up to a pasteuriser where it was raised to 145° F for 30 minutes and then rapidly cooled, to destroy 'all germs which threaten the human system'. The treated milk was then stored in a 1,000 gallon aluminium tank until drawn off for delivery. The Dairy's own artesian well ensured ample supplies of water for churn and bottle washing, should the city's mains ever fail. There was even a Reception Room where visiting school parties could listen to talks and view the Process Room from a balcony.

The Society now boasted the finest milk treatment facilities in the area and claimed that Co-operative Milk - at 2½d. a pint - was the purest and cheapest available. A propaganda leaflet, quoting leading academics, extolled the health-promoting qualities of what it described as *Nature's Most Perfect Food.*

The Department did indeed take its public health responsibilities seriously. Milk from over 200 East Riding farms was routinely tested for cleanliness and fat content. The Manager was entitled to visit any farm without warning to inspect the dairy herd, cowsheds and utensils. There were two bacteriologists on the staff, Miss Winifred Priestley and Mr. David Ralph (who later became the Dairy Manager). And from 1927 a bonus was paid to farmers who maintained high standards, while those with a poor record faced being de-listed.

The farmer with the best annual results was awarded a silver cup at a presentation tea in the Arcade Cafe, to which all the suppliers and their wives were invited. Taking place just before Christmas, this ceremony made a special day out for the farming community. The friendly rivalry engendered led to a remarkable improvement in milk quality, to the ultimate benefit of all consumers.

In the early days milk was sold loose and measured out into the customer's own jug or basin from a large metal can. The first experiment with bottled milk in 1924 had to be abandoned because members failed to return their used bottles promptly. It was tried again, more successfully, six years later. Filling the bottles and fitting their cardboard tops was done manually and the bottle washing equipment was the most primitive imaginable; it consisted of a brush contraption attached to a wall. Later the bottles were placed in cages that moved along a conveyor while water sprayed inside. The man who put the cages on at one end had to dash to the other end to turn them up to begin the rinsing process.

In those days any customer wanting bottled milk had to order it specially. One deliverer, who took his can and measures to Sutton by motorbike and sidecar, remembers the Dairy Manager Mr. Stansfield telling him to hide the bottles in his sidecar as they didn't want bottled milk to become too popular! Mr. Stansfield was for 25 years a most efficient and popular manager. A strict disciplinarian, he would instantly dismiss any employee caught smoking while on duty. Even so he was held in the highest esteem by Management, staff and members alike.

The Co-op milkman pushing his milk 'pram' became a familiar sight in the streets of Hull. There were 14 distribution depots where the roundsmen were based and the prams stored. Milk supplies arrived by lorry early each morning from which the prams were loaded up. Electric milk floats first made their appearance in 1954; each depot was then equipped to re-charge their batteries overnight. It took eight years to phase out the prams. In the country districts house-to-house deliveries were usually made by motor van. Heavy snowfalls meant headaches for the Department, for the prams became almost impossible to push along. The Labour Exchange sent unemployed men and youths to help out, which of course all added to the expense. But in really Arctic weather the Society was better placed than its competitors, being able to fall back on its shops to distribute the milk.

Unlike present-day roundsmen the Co-op milkmen sold only milk and cream. To save them having to keep detailed records a token system was used. Tokens, resembling small coins, could be obtained either from Co-op Grocery shops or Branch Travellers and exchanged for milk on the doorstep. Metal tokens were employed for Pasteurised Milk while plastic ones were used for Sterilised Milk (red and green) and for the Government's Free and Cheap Milk Scheme for children and nursing mothers (blue and white). Members received their dividend check when the tokens were bought.

The Dairy Office administered the token scheme and kept the accounts. Sheila Coates, who joined the staff there straight from school, remembers operating a machine called a spinner to count the thousands of tokens arriving daily in cloth bags from the depots. Her duties also extended to making up and sending out the depot wages. One unforgettable week she caused ructions by inadvertently putting the De

Grey Street wages into the De la Pole Avenue bag and vice versa!

When school milk was introduced the Co-op became the main supplier to Hull's council schools. Special bottles and filling plant were bought and drinking straws were supplied free of charge. In 1939 the evacuation of children from the urban area had a prejudicial effect on milk sales and an alternative outlet - the Glaxo factory at Driffield - had to be found for the surplus. From 1948 onwards customers could also buy Sterilised Milk supplied by the CWS Creameries at Bradford and Uttoxeter.

After the last war, the Dairy - which itself had merely suffered superficial damage - was the only building left standing in its area. Consequently the site attracted the attention of the post-war planners and in 1950 the Corporation exercised their powers of compulsory purchase. The Society, which had just spent a small fortune installing the latest equipment - including an aluminium foil capping machine, was forced to accept rental terms with a six month's termination clause. Fortunately the new landlords were prepared to allow the Dairy's vital work to continue while their plans for the area were being finalised.

By 1963 the Dairy was the Society's second largest department, with sales exceeding £1 million a year and an annual throughput of 3.6 million gallons. With the retail price fixed nationally and full dividend paid on every pint, members had a clear incentive to obtain all their milk from the Co-op.

In September 1966 the inevitable happened: the Society received notice to quit. After carefully considering the options open to them the Directors decided, with the greatest reluctance, to dispose of the entire milk business to their biggest competitor, the Hull-based Northern Dairies Ltd. It fell to the President, Mr. Fred Hall, to explain the decision to a special Members' Meeting on 21st November 1967.

Milk prams or 'dandies' outside the Gt. Thornton Street Dairy. Dairy Manager Mr. W.A. Stansfield is on the extreme right. The presence of so many female deliverers, and the fashions, suggest that this view dates from World War I.

Hull Co-op Milk Tokens: Brass tokens were used when summer prices operated and aluminium ones in winter. Milk was usually about a ha'penny cheaper during the summer.

Co-op Milk was extensively promoted as beneficial to health. This publicity float is parked on the Hull Corporation Field ready to take part in a May Day Parade.

Dr. W.M. Fryer (Medical Officer of Health) presenting the Hull Co-operative 'Clean Milk' Challenge Cup to Mr. Digby Cooke, a Beverley farmer, at a Yorkshire Show in the 1930s.

According to an Accountant's report the Society's plans to build a new dairy for £400,000 would not have been a viable proposition. Another proposal, to take milk wholesale either from the CWS or Northern Dairies and distribute it from a new depot, had also been assessed by experts but the costings had again come out on the wrong side.

The transfer, in January 1968, brought to an end a service used daily by over 30,000 customers. Towards the end Great Thornton Street had been supplying around 7,000 gallons of daily milk to the city, its suburbs and the towns of Beverley, Hornsea and Withernsea. 131 were employed on rounds plus 38 inside staff on bottling, pasteurising and office work. The Directors'

Report of March 1968 concluded: 'The sale of the business and vehicles resulted in a satisfactory sum accruing to the Society and the Directors were particularly pleased that Northern and Clover Dairies were able to absorb 133 members of the Dairy staff.'

However, our story of Co-op milk does not quite end there. In 1996 a rationalisation plan within the dairy industry saw it return to parts of East Yorkshire. Under a round-swapping agreement the Whitby-based Associated Co-operative Creameries began to supply the Bridlington and Driffield areas in place of Northern Foods, who simultaneously moved into some former Co-op territory in the Midlands.

NON-FOOD DEPARTMENTS

Premises:

19-23 Jarratt Street	D B T	1899-1907
24-5 Jarratt Street	F	1899-1917
Jameson Street	All	*1908-1941
		1947-1982
592 Hessle Road	D B T	1904-1915
266 Holderness Road	D B T	1905-1969
Bridlington, King Street	D B T	1913-1967
	F H	1913-1977
369-71 Hessle Road	D B T	1915-1965
Withernsea, Queen Street	D B T	1915-1971
	F H	1915-1982
469 Anlaby Road	D B T	1919-1922
Beverley, Toll Gavel	D B T	@ 1929-1972
Beverley Road/Fountain Rd.	F H	1941-1959
Pocklington, Market Street	D B T	@ 1956-1969
	F H	@ 1956-1982
Market Weighton, York Road	D B T	@ 1963-1972
	F H	@ 1963-1975
Leads Road	Disco	1973-1982
Bridlington, Chapel St.	F H	1977-1982
363-7 Hessle Road	Disco	1976-1981
369 Hessle Road	FF	1976-1981
257 Holderness Road	FF	1976-1982
260 Greenwood Avenue	FF	1977-1981
41-5 Beverley Road	Disco	1979-1982
Hessle, Swinegate	FF	1979-1982

Key:
D - Drapery, B - Boots, T - Tailoring, F - Furniture, H - Hardware,
FF - Factory Footwear
* Destroyed by enemy action. @ Date of transfer to Hull Soc'y.

Boot Repairing at:

7 Jarratt Street	1900-1907
Holland Street	1905-1958
Jameson Street	1907-1934
469 Anlaby Road	1919-1922
Little Albion Street	1934-1966
3-9 Hessle Road	1966-1968

Managers:

Drapery/Fashions etc: C.H. Gordon, A.P. Jobling, W.E. Martin, E. Secker, J.E. Bates, H. Cohen, M. Brown.
Footwear: W.H. Binks, C. Currins, H. Gibbons, C.E. Hey, C.F. Mears, G.F.A. Floyd, G. Regan, N. Webb.
Furnishing/Carpets/Hardware: C.H. Gordon, L. Stringer, F. Taylor, H.H. Bowness, D. Knappett, C. Walmsley, R.Westmorland.
Tailoring/Outfitting: W. Davies, J. Davies, C. Bowring, W. Godwin, H. Whitehead, C. Dawson, L. Barker, G. Patchett, R.S.Drax K.Kaye.
Electrical/TV & Radio: F.W. Henderson, F.C. Bentley, J. Barker.
Display: G. Frost, M. Turner.
Non-Food Trades Officer: F.W. Henderson.

Non-foods - Drapery, Footwear, Clothing, Hardware and Furnishings, though accounting for a minor share of overall trade, were important to the Society as it strove to become a 'universal provider'. At first, they were sold from the rooms above certain Grocery shops, albeit in a rather haphazard fashion. Hessle Road and Anlaby Road, for example, shared an assistant, one shop opening mornings; the other afternoons. But the shortage of space unduly restricted customers' choice while the dusty atmosphere associated with food shops tended to spoil the fine fabrics. When business was centralised at Jarratt Street in 1899, both service and trade improved considerably.

The opening of the new Central Premises in 1908, in a more prominent location in Jameson Street, was a proud moment for local Co-operators. The first phase housed the Gents' Boots, Outfitting and Drapery sections on the ground floor with Ladies' Boots, Millinery, Mantles (gowns) and Dressmaking on the first. Boots were made and repaired in the basement, while the light and airy top floor made ideal quarters for the Tailoring workrooms. A cash railway system, worked by electric motors and known as The Cable, was a novel feature of this store.

At Dairycoates the Society had a Cabinet Works where (to quote an early brochure) furniture was 'built to order by experienced workmen out of carefully-selected and well-seasoned timber, and all under Trade Union principles'. Re-painting and re-taping of venetian blinds, picture framing, polishing, upholstering, piano tuning, and garment cleaning and dyeing were just a few of the services offered. And twice daily a horse-drawn van visited every Grocery branch to collect and deliver an annual total of more than 20,000 boot repair jobs.

To help members plan their spending, it was important to offer credit. The first Drapery Club, opened in 1905, worked on a 20-weeks principle. Members paid a shilling a week for every pound's worth of goods supplied in advance. An interesting variation on the theme was the Ballot Club. Members again paid 1/- in the £, but the Office used to draw 20 names from a hat. Whoever was drawn first could collect their goods straight away, whereas the member unlucky enough to be drawn 20th had to wait until their club was nearly paid off. For the Society it was virtually risk-free, since the full cost was 'covered' in advance. Right up to the 1980s, the Hull Co-op employed a hardy team of Club Collectors who ventured out in all weathers, usually on bicycles, to collect the weekly payments from members' homes.

A horse-drawn Furniture van dating from the first decade of the 20th century. Notice how the Society missed no opportunity to promote Co-operative membership.

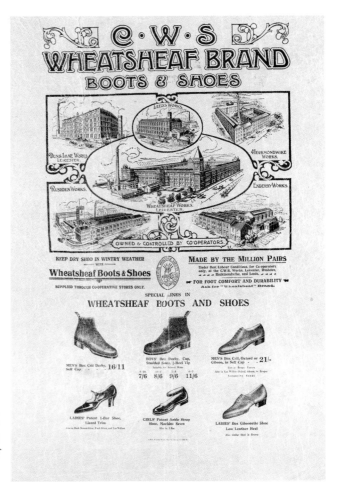

Printed wrapping paper in use, circa 1920s. Sketches of Co-op factories, with examples of their products, fostered the pride of ownership that helped to keep members loyal to their Stores (By courtesy of Mr. R. Lazenby).

A corner of the temporary post-war Store in Jameson Street (Picture by courtesy of Mrs S. Walker).

Defiant became one of the Co-op's greatest success stories when, in the interests of the consumer, it took on and defeated the mighty forces of private industry.

The handsome Royal Arcade building in King Street, Bridlington, opened by the Co-op in 1939. It contained a beautiful Adam ceiling which, at the request of local historians, was preserved in a splendid condition.

In 1915 the Society appointed its first Furnishing Manager. For nearly 30 years Mr. Leonard Stringer worked most enthusiastically, and with notable success, to build up his Department's reputation. Yet it is one of life's ironies that a manager's little idiosyncrasies tend to be recounted long after their business triumphs have faded from memory. Mr. Stringer often caused some amusement by taking his push-bike to work with him on the tram, in case he needed to make some house calls. He would park it on the driver's platform, safely out of the way of fellow passengers. But the trusty steed tended to be more trouble than it was worth, as time and again this little scenario unfolded later in the day:

LS to Junior Assistant: Go and fetch my bike, would you, I need to make some visits.

Assistant: Right you are, Mr. Stringer.

Assistant (returning later, looking puzzled): I can't seem to find it anywhere, Mr. Stringer.

LS: Then you'd better get yourself down to the tramsheds and get it back for me!

One of Mr. Stringer's former colleagues can still picture him delivering a wringer to a house off Holderness Road by man-handling it on to a tramcar outside the Store and then pushing it down the customer's street.

In 1924, shortly after public broadcasting began, the Hull Co-op became one of the first in Britain to open a Wireless Section. The product range also included gramophones, by then no longer the status symbol of only the rich. But the Co-op's early breakthrough in these new markets troubled the independent radio dealers. Arguing that its dividend represented unfair competition, in 1933 they managed to persuade the Radio Manufacturers' Association to cut off supplies to societies' stores unless they stopped paying it on sales of their products. The Co-op Movement's reaction, though, was hardly the one they had bargained for. Determined not to let private industry undermine one of its basic principles, it swiftly arranged for the CWS to launch an 'own-brand' radio set.

Marketed rather aptly under the Defiant label, the venture proved an instant success and in time a full range was developed, from small table-top sets to full-scale radiograms in beautiful teak cabinets made in the CWS Cabinet Works at Shirley. In later years the CWS was also well to the fore with television and Defiant became one of the industry's leading names, on a par with Philips, Ferguson and Bush.

In the 1930s, labour-saving appliances like electric cleaners, toasters and irons were unknown in the majority of East Yorkshire homes. But the enterprising Hull Co-op was keen to promote their uptake. On buying up the adjacent fire-ravaged Zimmerman's store in 1935, it turned the extra space on the first floor into a separate Electrical Section, headed by Mr. Charlie Cavill. Customers browsing around this showroom had two cylinder vacuum cleaners to choose from, both CWS-made - a standard model selling for £6/19/6d. (twice the then average weekly wage) and a leather-clad De Luxe version at 10 guineas. The latter had chrome end pieces and came packed in a dark wooden box, complete with a set of accessories. Jim Peddie, the Publicity Manager, organised a sales team to go round 'door-knocking' to promote these lines.

At one time the Society had no fewer than 15 electrical demonstrators at Jameson Street, employed on a commission basis by makers like Electrolux, Hoover and Servis to 'push' their respective products. To succeed in this job a ruthless competitive streak was needed. One saleswoman in particular was widely regarded as the finest in the business. While at her pitch in the Arcade one day, she engaged in conversation with a lady who was making her way to the Funeral Office to order a headstone for her late husband's grave. By the time she had finished her patter, the lady was firmly convinced that her Dear Departed would have much preferred her to treat herself to a new vacuum cleaner and had changed her plans completely!

Memories of the fine old pre-war Store abound among Hull folk. Many women can still remember buying their clothes from a Miss Smith who was in charge of gowns and millinery; people used to refer to her as The Duchess because of her regal demeanour. Another abiding memory is the thrill of seeing Father Christmas pop out of a chimney on the roof and wave merrily to the crowds gathered on the pavement opposite. The new Store, too, was always noted for its Santa's Grotto; indeed, in a newspaper survey, it was once voted the best in Yorkshire. Year after year the Society's talented Display team and Works personnel co-operated to produce some imaginative sets, ranging from the traditional Lapland sleigh ride to, on one occasion, the Magic Roundabout of TV fame and, on another, a live animal zoo. The latter reportedly caused a commotion one morning when the sales staff arrived to find the snakes missing from their tanks! The 1968 festive season turned out to be the busiest period in the history of the Store. A record 49,000 children visited the Grotto and toy sales were so brisk that General Office staff had to be drafted in to help behind the counters.

The Society operated Non-Food branches in a number of East Riding towns. Making a go of a 'Branch Drapery' called for a special all-round flair for, with such a limited market, gauging accurately the likely demand for, say, each size of shoe or ladies' corset was nearly impossible; the stock all too easily degenerated into a higgledy-piggledy mass of unsaleable oddments. One person who appeared to have the necessary qualities was Grace Wells, who for 30 years presided at Beverley. 'Strict but very fair' is how Joyce Eaton (nee Lewis) recalls her boss's management style: 'As soon as Miss Wells arrived it was obvious she was a real businesswoman. She insisted on clearing out every scrap of old stock and making a completely fresh start. Her office stood at the end of the long counter running down one side of the shop and if a customer left and your till hadn't rung, you were called in for such a

questioning. What did she want? Did you show her such and such? Had you been upstairs to see if we had anything else? Only when she was satisfied that you'd done everything possible to make a sale would she simply say "very well" and that was that.' With Miss Wells at the helm, the fortunes of this branch went from strength to strength.

Over the years the Hull Co-op forged a number of links with the sporting world. When Hull Kingston Rovers appeared in the Rugby League Cup Final in 1964, the Menswear Department was invited to supply the team with their off-the-field outfits. Bill Fallowfield, the League Secretary, later 'phoned through to say that, in his opinion, HKR were the best turned-out team ever seen at Wembley and offered the Society the privilege of dressing the Great Britain team for their Australian tour. Weeks of frantic activity followed, led by manager Ray Drax and assisted by the Head of Bespoke Tailoring, Ken Humphreys. It was a far from simple task; clearly, to represent the nation, every detail had to be just right, but rugby players are not the easiest men in the world to fit! As it was impracticable to visit every player at his home club, arrangements were made to notify the Society whenever the squad were called together for training so that someone could be there with a tape measure. The Society was highly complimented on the outcome and, as a gesture of appreciation, was allowed to display the actual World Cup in one of the Jameson Street windows.

The association with the city's Rugby clubs was a matter of considerable pride but was not at the expense of the 'round ball' variety. In the 1950s the legendary Stanley Matthews visited the Store with his collection of International Caps and his own CWS-made football boots. 'As soft and light as a pair of slippers' is how former Menswear Manager Ken Kaye remembers them. Then, in 1967, the Society appointed the great Raich Carter - the ex-Hull City player-manager who swept the Tigers to a peak of

Popular entertainer George Formby putting in an appearance at a Co-op Fashion Show in the Jameson Street Store (Picture by courtesy of Mrs S. Walker).

Some of the backroom staff rarely seen by the customers: Florence Clarkson (far left) with the Tailoring Workroom staff in the 1950s (Picture by courtesy of Mrs J.M. Poskitt).

national prominence that, alas, has never been repeated since - to manage perhaps the most extensive Sports Department Hull has ever seen, complete with indoor practice golf range. But, like so many Hull Co-op ventures of that era, it was probably too far ahead of its time to produce the returns expected of it.

In the 1970s the Society began to get criticism that its Jameson Street Store wasn't matching the keen prices of Comet and other discount traders that had moved into Hull. The Non-Food Trades Officer, Mr. Frank Henderson, came to the opinion that, although unable to offer discount prices in a department store, the Co-op could in fact set up, in suitable premises, a discount operation of its own, with prices to not only meet the competition but, in many instances, beat it. And so, in 1973, Hull Disco was born. The venture proved a huge success and was later expanded while the Society continued to trade quite satisfactorily at department store prices in the city centre. That CRS eventually abandoned the concept merely reflected its incompatibility with their then 'store profile' rather than any lack of viability.

At the time of writing local Co-operators were eagerly looking forward to the opening of 'Homeworld' at Kingswood, marking the return of Co-operative Non-food trading to the Hull area after an absence of 15 years.

COAL DEPARTMENT.

Managers:

T. Lilley
W. Bayford
E. Lee
W.E.Watts
G.A. Stainton

Main Depots:

Cannon St./Gibson St.	1897-1952
Alexandra Dock	1897-1925
Neptune Street	1901-1915
Burleigh Street	1905-1952
Dairycoates	1907-1952
Ella Street	1908-1952
Sculcoates Lane	1936-1966
Calvert Lane	1940-1978

Coal Depots also at Howden, Bridlington, Withernsea, Hornsea, Beverley and Pocklington.

Keeping the home fires burning was a major preoccupation for the householder in the days when every home had a solid fuel grate, and some had three or four. The Management Committee therefore gave the development of the domestic coal trade a priority second only to food.

The Society set up its first Coal Depots in 1897, the supplies for which were all procured from carefully-selected Yorkshire collieries using the buying power of the mighty CWS. Within ten years the annual throughput had grown to 20,000 tons; regular customers were enjoying a discount of 8d. a ton and a Coal Club allowed members to buy their fuel on credit.

The Co-op's unique network of ordering points - its own Grocery shops - avoided the need for expensive coal offices in all parts of the town. It was the branch errand boy's job to cycle to the nearest Coal Depot each morning with the previous day's orders. Any lad overlooking this essential task was likely to get a 'clip round the ear' from his manager!

Fuel prices stayed remarkably constant between the wars. So much so in fact that each Grocery branch displayed a wooden board outside on which the price of each grade of coal was not chalked but permanently painted. This happy state of affairs lasted until supply restrictions were imposed in the 1940s.

Deliveries were made by dray-men operating horse-drawn rulleys from the Society's several stables. Herbert Day gave this account of life as a Co-op dray-man in the 1930s: Work in the stables began at 7.30 a.m. when each driver groomed and harnessed his horse and yoked it to a vehicle ready to move out of the yard by 8 o'clock. Each day a dray-man was required to deliver three loads weighing a total of seven tons.

At the coal yard fillers worked in pairs to shovel coal into bags. The dray-man held a sack on the scales and when it was filled to the correct weight they hoisted it on to his back. He carried it over to his rulley, setting it down carefully on the platform. There was a knack in placing four rows of up to ten bags in such a way as to create a safe load.

The first load, containing 32 ten-stone bags, was delivered to customers living close to the depot. The second, of 40 bags, was taken further afield. The dray-man then returned his vehicle to the depot where he unyoked his horse and led it to the stable, arriving by one o'clock. An hour later he would set off for another load, usually destined for one of the housing estates on the outskirts of the city - the longest haul for the horse. The delivery men were checked in and out of the depot by the yard foreman and carried a note book in which to record all the streets visited, together with order forms bearing each customer's name and address, the grade of coal and amount ordered. There were at least eight grades with different names which they had to memorise and learn to distinguish.

Herbert reckoned it was almost impossible to deliver seven tons of coal in the scheduled eight hours. Instead of overtime pay, men were given time off in lieu and casual workers taken on to make up any shortfall. But in the summer months when the coal trade was slack, even regular dray-men faced being stood off and their horses were rested on one of the Society's farms.

In 1924 a steam wagon was experimented with for coal deliveries. It was soon found unsuitable. The platform was so far from the ground that the coalmen had to climb on board to fetch bags down, which all slowed up the job and added to the cost. Then, around 1930 Mr. Horace Plant,

the Traffic Manager, introduced a three-wheeled motor vehicle called a Scammac. It too was considered a failure. It was awkward to manoeuvre in Hull's rear tenfoots and time was lost because the driver had to climb in and out of a cab, unlike a horse which could be led from gate to gate. The horse seemed set to reign supreme for many years to come. However, in 1945 the Society began to assemble a fleet of Karrier Bantam tractors and trailers for coal deliveries; three years later the transition to motorised transport was complete.

In the austerity years, especially during the notorious winter of 1947, the Department was plagued with problems. There was simply not enough coal being mined to satisfy demand and the Government's quota scheme, which was intended to ensure fair shares for all, proved hopelessly inadequate. The Society received scores of complaints but was powerless to help. Added to this there was a desperate shortage of labour and for a time Italian Prisoners of War had to be employed on deliveries.

Coal yards in the Hull area were owned by the railway authorities who leased them to the merchants. In 1966 the reception and distribution of all coal was centralised on Calvert Lane where mechanical handling and bag-filling equipment was installed to save on labour costs and eliminate the back-breaking job of shovelling coal.

In the early-1960s Coal sales peaked at £500,000 a year. But a long slow decline loomed ahead as families switched over to cleaner forms of heating. Hull's vast new estates became smokeless zones, while the latest multi-storey flats were 'all-electric'. Trade also suffered whenever a Grocery branch closed down; experiments with hawking coal in the affected areas met with only limited success. In 1978 the Board decided to sell the remnants of this once thriving business to PD Fuels.

Gibson Street Coal Yard, 1933. The Hull Co-op's own fleet of private owner railway wagons plied between colliery and depot. Requisitioned by the authorities in World War II, they were handed over to the British Transport Commission on nationalisation of the railways. The Society received £3,069 worth of Government Stock as compensation. Note all coal bags were filled by hand - a back-breaking job.

Horse-drawn coal rulley setting forth from Holmes Street depot. All the Society's rulleys were built to order by Chapman Bros. of Wincolmlee.

FUNERAL FURNISHING DEPARTMENT

Managers:

F.W. Wright
A. Hindley
C.E. Collinson

Funeral Homes:

84 Charles Street	1936-1966
23 Hutt Street	1944-1976
344 Holderness Road	1964-
228 Boothferry Road	1987-

Workshops: Hall Street 1936-47; 104 Coltman Street 1947-64. Monumental Masonry: Cottingham, 240 Hallgate; Bridlington, Brooklands Road.
Manager's Residence: 436 Anlaby Road.

It was perhaps only natural that an organisation aspiring to cater for its members' needs from the cradle to the grave should seek to provide a Funeral service. In appointing a manager to run its new business the Society could not have chosen better than Mr. Fred Wright, a well-known Cottingham joiner/undertaker and one of only a few qualified embalmers in the Hull area.

The headquarters were set up in Charles Street where the Vicar of Sculcoates hallowed a Chapel of Repose in April 1936. The first order came from a Cottingham member and the story goes that Mr. Marshall, the General Manager, was so excited when the call came through that he dashed for a tape measure and insisted on accompanying Mr. Wright on his home visit.

Mr. Wright needed a receptionist to look after the Rest Rooms and Mr. Marshall offered him Ruth Clarke, a ledger clerk in the General Office. It was a demanding role, for the place was often so cramped that she had to work miracles to keep the various mourning parties apart. After her first fortnight Miss Clarke was therefore relieved to learn that her new boss had reported back to Mr. Marshall that she was '100 per cent'.

The Department quickly gained a good reputation, with the volume of business fully justifying the investment. As might be expected the staff had to cope with many harrowing incidents, especially during wartime when sometimes whole families were lost. At the height of the Hull Blitz the Co-op conducted 80 funerals in a single week. Fortunately there were some lighter moments too. In those days it was common practice to lay the deceased in their coffin in the family home so that relatives and friends could call round to pay their respects. According to Miss Clarke there was one occasion when 'we learnt that the client was quite satisfied with the service but most disappointed with the coffin. She thought it would have matched her furniture. It made us wonder if the lady intended to keep it there for ever. Mr. Wright was quite concerned and rushed straight round to make amends'.

The Funeral Director's residence at 436 Anlaby Road also doubled as a branch enquiry office. But members could request the service at any Co-op store throughout East Yorkshire and be sure of prompt attention, an important consideration in the days when few families had a telephone at home. Another advantage was the availability of allied services through the Society's many departments. Catering, either at home or in a private suite, could be arranged through the Manageress of the Arcade Cafe. And according to a 1938 brochure: 'Mourning wear for ladies and gentlemen is a speciality of our Tailoring and Dress Departments, Jameson Street. None are more fitted and able to meet the sudden demand for mourning wear than your own Society.'

The Department engaged its own coffin-makers, also a team of stonemasons, who won a contract to affix a granite tablet to the base of the King William III statue in the city's Market Place. So far as is known this was the only time in its history that the Hull Co-op had any business dealings with Royalty!

The specialist motor vehicles were maintained

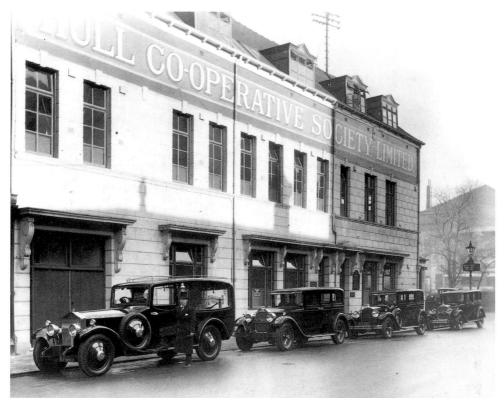

The Society's Funeral fleet outside the Jarratt Street Offices in the 1930s. Mr. Fred Wright the Manager is standing by the Rolls Royce hearse (Picture by courtesy of Mr. C.E. Collinson).

The Coltman Street Funeral Workshops team in the 1950s:
Standing (left to right) - Stuart 'Lofty' Scott, Charles Collinson, Don Hardy, Herbert Tunley, George Clark, Fred Clayton, Reg Shields, Neville Woods, Albert Wiles.
Seated - Ron Hutchinson, Ted Kirk, Fred Wright (Departmental Manager), Les Dobbs, Brian Briggs (Picture by courtesy of Mr. C.E. Collinson).

by Gills' Garage on Holderness Road until 1952 when the property and fleet were taken over by the Society. On 20th April 1964, after extensive re-development, these premises were officially opened by Dr. Alexander Hutchison (the Medical Officer of Health) and dedicated by Canon Stevenson as the city's new Co-operative Funeral Home. Acknowledged as one of the finest in the North, it included a chapel for 40 mourners, eight rest rooms with satin-covered beds, a reception area, offices, monumental showrooms, garages, workshops, a florist's shop and an employee's flat. The public areas were tastefully decorated and carpeted, the aim being to replace the rather stark atmosphere of the funeral parlours of yesteryear with the best possible 'home from home' bereavement care. To complete the picture, Vanden Plas Princess limousines were bought to replace the original Rolls Royce's, these being succeeded in their turn by a fleet of the very latest Daimlers.

After the Hull Society merged with CRS in 1981 a range of Pre-payment Funeral Plans was introduced. By planning and paying for their funeral in advance, many people can gain peace of mind, knowing that the burden will not fall upon their loved ones when the time comes.

The year 1986 saw the retirement of Mr. Charles Collinson, after 45 years service, the last 20 as the Department's Manager. As a youngster Charlie had entered the profession more by chance than by choice. He was employed as a warehouse boy in the basement of the Pharmacy Department at Jameson Street until that fateful night when the building was destroyed in the Blitz. The next day all the staff were called to the Institute to try to fix them up with other work. With many of the city's phone lines down, the Funeral Department needed two cycle lads to run errands, taking official forms to the cemeteries to notify them of people lost in the air raids. Charlie and his pal Walt Fussey (a future Manager of Withernsea Drapery) were chosen.

Mr. Wright quickly spotted Charlie's potential and encouraged him to train for embalming and coffin-making, and at 18 he became the youngest apprentice in the country to qualify as an embalmer. Soon he was working his way up the ladder, becoming Foreman at the Coltman Street Workshops in 1956 and Assistant to the Manager two years later, before taking on the managerial role in 1966. He was Secretary and thrice President of the Hull & District Association of Funeral Directors, and in 1985 enjoyed momentary 'stardom' by appearing, driving a funeral car, in the John Cleese film *Clockwise,* parts of which were filmed in Hull.

Among the many colleagues Charlie recalls working with (as well as those shown in the photograph) are: Herbert Gee, Ossie North, David Fletcher, Neville Brown, John Grantham, Joyce Barton, Mrs Fox, Mrs Read, Joan Broadwell and Winnie Ireland.

During its 60 year existence the Hull Co-operative Funeral Service has developed a reputation second to none in its profession and local Co-operators are justifiably proud of the standards achieved. It continues to go about its work, quietly and efficiently, of rendering the best possible service to those who entrust it with their confidence.

THE GENERAL OFFICE

Secretary:

W.H. Taylor
K.H. Whitehead
S. Lamb
W.J. Payling
J.M. James
A. Mair
Hy. Ferguson FCIS
Wm. Gratrix FCRA
S. Marshall JP FCIS FLAA
F. Cant
A. Barnes
J.D. Macpherson FCCA (General Secretary)

General Manager:

S. Marshall JP FCIS FLAA
A. Barnes
H.C. Greening

Chief Executive/Secretary

J.D. Macpherson FCCA
J.R. Brown CSD:

201 Hessle Road	1890-1891
11 Wilton Terrace, Holderness Rd.	1891-1898
7 Jarratt Street	1898-1902
26 Jarratt Street	1902-1961
2 Jameson Street	1961-1981

The General Office was the hub of the Society's operations. By 1902 it had taken up a prominent corner site in the city centre. Its work was organised into three sections: 'A' Department (Accounts), on the first floor, paid the merchants' accounts and the employees' wages; collected debts; produced the Society's official accounts and kept records of its extensive property portfolio. 'B' Department (the Bank or *Cashier's*) staffed the public counter; handled share, loan and penny bank transactions; kept the register of members and organised the twice-yearly dividend pay out. It was on the ground floor. 'C' Department (Check Office), on the top floor, kept records of all the shops' takings and tallied up each member's purchases in order to calculate their dividend.

When selecting junior staff, preference was generally given to the children of loyal Co-op members. Each applicant faced a daunting test in arithmetic, spelling and handwriting to establish their suitability for the position of Office Boy or Girl. Entering the portals of 26 Jarratt Street for her test one Saturday in 1912, Doris Compston was crestfallen to find the top girl in her school already there. She knew at once that she stood no chance of being taken on. But the Society must have kept her details on file, for six weeks later a letter arrived offering her the next vacancy.

Doris described her 13 years at the Co-op as

some of the happiest of her life: 'I started in the Check Office on four shillings a week, sitting around a big table with nine other girls. We had to add up members' checks and sort them into share number order with a wooden frame (divided into 2" squares) balanced on our lap. At half past ten each morning I had to make a cup of Bovril for the big boss (Mr. Gratrix); for this he rewarded me with a Christmas box of 7/6d!' Doris later progressed on to ledger work in Accounts. The ledgers were so heavy, she recalled, that the male clerks were expected to take it in turns to carry them between the shelves and their female colleagues' desks.

Jean Marshall's first duty, on joining the staff in 1925, was to learn how to operate the Society's Telephone Switchboard. It was a primitive affair, with just two lines to the Corporation Exchange and a direct link to certain branch shops. A little tab dropped down to indicate which shop was ringing in and to connect the call the operator had to plug in a cord. Internal communications, however, relied on a speaking tube: 'To transmit a message from the ground floor to the attic you pulled out a stopper and blew down the hole, which sounded a shrill whistle in the Check Office. The voice of the person answering came through loud and clear, for everyone to hear, so private conversations were impossible.'

At the age of 16 Jean transferred to the Typing Pool. Presently, with some impressive shorthand qualifications behind her (190 words per minute Pitman's), her career took a big leap forward when she was appointed Personal Secretary to Mr. Samuel Marshall (no relation), the General Manager. Her duties in this key position were many and varied. Once a week Mr. Marshall would dictate the Management Committee proceedings into his Ediphone for Jean to transcribe in her best long hand into the impressively leather-bound minute books. Occasionally she was sent to take notes at Court cases in which the Co-op was interested. But her most macabre assignment was to make a

The Society's imposing headquarters - 26 Jarratt Street. Twice a year, for 60 years, thousands of members passed through its doors to draw their divi. The property was demolished in 1975, save for the historic portico of the Co-operative Institute, which is protected by a preservation order. In the 1830s this had formed part of the Hull School of Medicine.

A 'happy snap' taken at the General Office Christmas Party in 1953. On the front row are Mr. F. Cant - Secretary (third from left), Mr. W. Kirk - President (third from right) and Mr. A. Barnes - General Manager (far right).

The 100ft. long banking counter in the new Jameson Street Store. It was designed to cope with the divi week crowds but, by the time it came into use, they were no more (Picture by courtesy of Innes Studios).

The Hull and East Riding Co-op Office staff gathered in March 1975 to wish their Chief Executive, 'Mr. Mac' (Mr. J.D. Macpherson), (far right) a happy retirement.

verbatim record of a Funeral Directors' Conference during which a corpse was wheeled into the room and a lady embalmer performed a practical demonstration in front of her eyes. The party then adjourned to the Imperial Hotel for a sumptuous meal!

Jean remembers the Office as a quiet, industrious place where the discipline was strict but fair. 'Our bosses worked hard and expected us to do the same. Smoking was banned and there were no tea breaks. Mind you, I used to make money for Rec. Club funds by selling CWS biscuits surreptitiously from my stationery cupboard,' she admits. 'Mr. Marshall wouldn't tolerate any fraternising. So the male and female lunch breaks were staggered by five minutes and girls couldn't enter the lift if a man was in. But his policy wasn't a success because at least four couples in the Office married, myself included.' In 1940 Jean married Bill Oxley who became the Society's Chief Clerk. Though her paid service had to end, the couple continued to help with Recreation Club events and later ran the Retired Employees' Association together for over 21 years.

No description of the Office would be complete without reference to Mr. Marshall - 'SM the GM' as he styled himself - a man of scrupulous honesty and total dedication to the Society. He routinely worked long hours, often spending his Saturday afternoons touring the Jameson Street Store, where his presence was sure to keep the staff on their mettle. Though involved in the weightiest of business matters, he had a keen eye for those little details, the attention to which marks out the better-run organisation from the rest. Here is an extract from one of his regular Office Bulletins to all the staff:

'A few days ago we inspected some handcarts sent in for repair. They were simply terrible, and it must have been very hard work for the boys to pull them through the streets. The carts had not had grease or oil on the axles for many months. Some had been provided with costly ball-bearing axles and it was a wicked shame to see such neglect. Will you please get your juniors to see to such matters? For a little attention now and again will save the Society pounds in expense, and if we cannot increase sales we can surely try to keep down expenses.'

To parody an old saying, Mr. Marshall clearly believed that for want of a little oil a Society could be lost.

Ex-Hull Grammar School boy Reg Kemp started as an Office Boy in 1926 on 15/- a week, attending evening classes at Hull College of Commerce to enhance his skills. His abilities were soon recognised for he was entrusted with writing up the Purchases Day Book, a sure sign in those days that one had 'arrived'. Reg recalls: 'The accounts clerks either perched on high stools or stood at tall wooden desks with sloping tops. We all used pens with replaceable nibs and to get a fresh nib you had to approach no less a person than the Assistant Secretary, Mr. Freddie Cant. The procedure seems laughable today, but before issuing one he would say, "Let me see your old one first, Kemp"'.

Twice a year the Office staff could earn a little extra by taking home batches of stock sheets to price up with the aid of a Pears Ready Reckoner. In similar fashion, members' interest and dividends had to be calculated and posted to the share ledgers. The Society paid a bonus of between ½d. and 2d. per sheet or per ledger page, depending on the complexity of the task. One-time Death Benefits Clerk, Mary Hellings, remembers new starters having to learn by heart the numbers of all the branch shops, a task that grew progressively harder as the Society expanded. A 1960s recruit had to identify some 90 Grocery and 60 Butchery branches in this way. But once memorised the knowledge stayed with you for life. Some ex-employees (including the writer) can still reel off the entire list or point out a Co-op building and quote its branch number.

Like most workplaces the Office had its share of 'characters'. None more so perhaps than the talented Jim Glasby, who loved to compose bits of poetry and humorous doggerel, sometimes about his colleagues! And when recounting Office life in the 1950s and '60s the name of Miss Gibson invariably crops up. Always referred to as Miss Gibson - never by her first name (Grace) - this redoubtable lady, attired in businesslike green overalls, ran the Check Office. Any girl joining the Jarratt Street staff initially came under her strict regime. 'Superb preparation for the Army' is how one remembers the experience. 'We weren't allowed to talk while working and any male visitors were watched like a hawk to make sure there was no fraternising!' Yet the girls gained an excellent grounding in office practice and Section Heads needing new staff would draw them from the Check Office knowing that they would always be first-class employees.

In the 1970s, when the writer joined the staff, electronic data processing was making inroads into the routines traditionally performed by the clerks. Even so more than 80 were still employed at the then Jameson Street headquarters. It was a place of notable camaraderie and most of the senior staff - including Reg Kemp (Chief Clerk), Bert Savage (Chief Cashier), Jack May (Accountant), Ray Abbey (Credit), Cyril Gardham (Sales), Selwyn Giles (Bank) and Dick Charlton (Personnel Manager) - had either come up through the shops or spent all their life in a Co-op Office; consequently they knew the business inside out.

A highspot of Office life was a gigantic raffle, drawn by the Chief Executive on the final afternoon before Christmas. This pleasant little tradition had started in the early 1950s, later being kept going by an Office Social Committee comprising two long-serving employees, June Gibson and John Bell, and other helpers. The staff paid a shilling a week to fund this treat, plus an annual social evening, two events that no one wanted to miss.

During 1982, after the merger with CRS, all administrative work was transferred to a Regional Office at Barnsley. However the CRS headquarters have since relocated to Rochdale, the birthplace of the Co-op Movement.

TRAFFIC AND ENGINEERING DEPARTMENT

Managers:

G. Lee
J. Fenton
W. Dowley
W.H. Shepherdson
H. Plant
S. Anson
N. Perkins

Premises:

Symons Street	1905-1968
Holmes Street	1920-1958
Parrott St./Tomlinson St.	1921-1931
Boothferry Road	1941-1968
Hessle (Northfield)	1942-1968
Holderness Road	1952-1964
Ryde Avenue	1958-1981

Branch Stables/Garages: Dairycoates, Nornabell Street, Main Street, Howden, Bridlington (Quay Road, West Street and Brett Street), Greenwich Avenue, Pocklington.

An efficient transport service was vital to the Hull Co-op, involved as it was in distributing such a variety of goods. For some fifty years the Horse Transport Section was the Society's mainstay. Its headquarters in Symons Street housed 21 dray-horses, with another five based at Nornabell Street and seven more at Dairycoates. Delivering coal, transferring branch orders from the Osborne Street Warehouse and leading flour to the Bakery from the CWS Mill were the principal tasks. The latter, the Section's heaviest daily duty, required a double-horse dray, longer and wider than a normal one-horse vehicle. It was loaded with 80 ten-stone bags, placed upright in two tiers. Up to four of these 5-ton loads had to be conveyed every working day.

Horse transport was not without its problems of course. Receiving reports of two accidents in 1919, the Coal & Stables Sub-Committee agreed to send ten shillings to 'the man who stopped our horse in Waterloo Street when it ran away'. Another time they learnt of a horse pulling its rulley on to a bed of wallflowers in Ella Street after shying at a passing engine. 'The attendants to be remonstrated with for their neglect and carelessness,' the Minutes sternly pronounced.

Even in the 1930s horse driving in the city was no mean feat, given the speed of motor traffic and the hazards of manoeuvring a double-shafted dray between the kerb and the tramlines. The old Drypool Bridge was a notorious bottle-neck, especially when a bus was approaching. Even so, for Herbert Day, the job had its high spots: 'Every summer the Society held an outdoor Gala and, to convey members and their children, we laid on a procession of our horse-vehicles. Some of them carried displays advertising various products sold in our shops. The horses' polished harness and plaited manes and tails made a splendid sight, with their brasses all glistening in the sunshine as we went along.'

The first motor van was acquired in 1910 for making deliveries from the Jameson Street Store; it was quickly followed by another to speed the despatch of bread and cakes. Ten years later a steam traction engine was trialled. Mainly deployed on collecting produce from East Riding farms, even this proved troublesome at times, the police occasionally pulling it up for smoking in the street.

It was Mr. Shepherdson, in the 1920s, who greatly expanded the petrol fleet. To him went the distinction of being the Society's first manager to be granted a 'company car'. Apparently, a Guildswoman, who had heard about this at the Members' Meeting, once flagged him down at a bus stop and demanded a ride into town in what she insisted on calling the

Co-op Car!

Albion petrol lorries formed the bulk of the heavy goods fleet from the 1930s onwards; Mr. Horace Plant, the then manager, favoured them for their low running costs and exceptional longevity. Unlike today's highly-standardised commercial fleets, the Society's other rolling stock comprised a somewhat motley collection of vans and trucks - Austin, Bedford, Morris and Ford makes all being represented. A team of six motor mechanics based at Holmes Street kept them on the road. For the drivers, the daily routine mainly involved delivering bread and meat to the shops, milk to the outlying Dairy depots, and furnishings to customers' homes.

As motor transport improved, the Horse Section lost the contracts to deliver groceries and flour; some empty stalls appeared at Symons Street. But the trend was momentarily reversed in the last war, when hostilities at sea curtailed petrol imports and motors were requisitioned. Another Stable was opened on Boothferry Road (near the Three Tuns), fitted out with cast-iron stalls acquired from Tranby Croft, the great house once owned by the shipping magnate, Arthur Wilson. To minimise the risk of loss, a fleet dispersal policy was practised, motors being parked up overnight at Westella, close to the manager's home. Seeing them pass by each morning in one piece no doubt reassured Mr. Plant. Mattresses were often carried so that the drivers and their families could sleep out in the country in relative safety. A number of women drivers were taken on and, to conserve precious petrol, a couple of vehicles used on the Bridlington run were converted to operate on producer-gas by burning a special solid fuel known as Progasite in cylinders fitted behind the cab.

When peace returned, the modernisation drive resumed in earnest and in March 1948 the remaining horses and rulleys were sold by auction. The *Hull Times* described the event: 'There was a large attendance including many

The Hull Co-operative vehicle fleet lined up outside Holmes Street Garage around 1920. Model T Fords and Daimlers are much in evidence.

Driver Tom Pearson preparing to deliver a load of CWS Flour, with Albion lorry no.51 (1934-55). At one time the HCS possessed 180 vehicles - one of the largest fleets in East Yorkshire - all smartly turned out in maroon livery with gold signage.

Holderness farmers. Sets of heavy harness made from £15 to £20; bridles up to £7, reins to 37/6d. and collars to £8/10/-. The rulleys were keenly competed for and made from £77 to £115. The rulley horses, their ages ranging from 7 years upwards, made from 35 to 46 guineas.' For the dray-men, many of whom had formed a lifelong attachment to their beloved animals, it was an exceedingly sad time.

Operating across a largely rural area, the Traffic staff faced numerous headaches in winter. Like most people of a certain age, motor-fitter Harry Plaxton has vivid memories of the frightful winters of 1947/8 and 1962/3, when the roads over the Yorkshire Wolds disappeared under 10-15 foot snowdrifts, halting all vehicular movement. The morning after the first blizzards the Garage 'phone was red-hot with calls from snowbound drivers wanting assistance. After loading up a 2-ton lorry with shovels, snow-shoes, tow-ropes, sandwiches and flasks of tea - and (to improve road-holding) a few sacks of sugar or whatever other ballast was to hand - Harry bravely ventured forth to search for bread vans and milk lorries stranded all over the Riding. Such missions were not always entirely successful, but welcome help might be rendered to other stricken drivers along the way. Trying to reach two Co-op wagons buried on Arras Hill, Harry and his mate Norman Perkins once dug out a shooting brake belonging to one of Hull's 'captains of industry', who promptly went home and fetched them hot coffee, cakes and a tot of whisky for their trouble! Another time, on calling at a lonely cottage for water for an Albion's radiator, they found the occupants in a state of distress. Their pantry was empty. Without further ado, pillow cases were found and stuffed with fresh loaves from the bread van, and trays of pastries and pies handed over, knowing full well the Bakery Manager would not have disapproved.

At the end of their working life, two Hull Co-op Albions were rescued by enthusiasts for preservation: RH 8059 (no.15 in the fleet), a flat plaform lorry built in 1932, and JRH 821 (no. 132), a 1947 canvas-topped lorry. 'Old no.15' (as she was affectionately known) was destined for a transport museum on the South Coast. As she had languished unused in the garage for some time, the new owners thought it prudent to have her towed down by a more youthful Land Rover. By coincidence, one of the Garage men was travelling home along the Great North Road and happened to see the convoy go past. The irony was that, instead of being towed, no.15 was in fact hauling the Land Rover, which had given up the ghost a few miles out of Hull! No.15 went on to a glorious retirement, touring France and winning prizes at various rallies, before settling down at the museum.

The Hull Co-op sold the Holmes Street Garage to the CWS in 1958 and moved into the former Tarran Industries' pre-cast flooring works in Ryde Avenue. But after the merger with CRS, all transport resources were centralised away from Hull, rendering a local depot superfluous.

WORKS DEPARTMENT

Managers:

J.W. Reynolds
W.E. Owst
A.P. Broughton
J. Ebbatson
G. Bayes
N. Perkins (Services Controller)

Premises

Gibson Street	1915-1924
Fern Street	1924-1971
Ryde Avenue	1971-1981

In May 1903 the Management Committee decided that 'as much as possible general property maintenance work be executed by direct labour'. John Reynolds was appointed Working Joiner and so began an important branch of the Society. Many well-built shops bear testimony to his efficiency as a builder. One of the first projects tackled was the Central

Emporium which, despite immense problems with Hull's notoriously unstable subsoil, was completed within a year. To make suitable foundations, old tramway metals were cut up and embedded in a thick mass of concrete.

By the 1920s the Department was responsible for virtually all the Society's joinery, bricklaying, electrical and painting needs, as well as vehicle body-building and maintaining shop handcarts and tills. Even rodent control came within the remit, if this Sub-Committee Minute is anything to go by: 'Committee noted rats giving trouble at Walliker Street. They feed under the Grocery and then go across to West Park for fun and recreation. Steps to be taken to have them poisoned.'

Hardwood standards were bought in bulk from Barchard's timber yard and expertly cut, planed and shaped into shop counters, wall fixtures and showcases. This was the responsibility of Foreman Joiner Walt Daddy, a first-class joiner, along with Fred Jordan, an expert in working mahogany, and Herbert Kilvington, who loved his oak. Huge sycamore logs, up to 30' long, were left to season for several years before being sawn up to meet a steady demand for cutting blocks for butcher's shops. And ash - being a supple wood - was fashioned into frames for wagons, over which a canvas cover could be draped.

The Painting Section always had a hectic schedule, with mahogany counter tops to polish, shelving to stain, decorative tilework to fix in Provisions sections, and regular attention to be given on rota to hundreds of property exteriors. Brown and buff were the standard hand-mixed shop colours pre-war - rather drab perhaps, but 'serviceable' was doubtless the view taken then. As the Society expanded, the skills of the Electrical Section were in great demand not only for new installations but also to keep all the plant and machinery functioning efficiently at the Bakery, Dairy, Pork Factory and Boot Repair Workshop.

During the 1930s the Department built several shops to the designs of its then manager, Mr. Bill Owst. By all accounts Mr. Owst was a stickler for timekeeping and tea and smoking breaks were definitely not favoured. After an hour or two in the dusty sawmill the men would be longing for a brew and one can imagine the relief when Mr. Owst finally announced he was going on a site visit. Once his bike was safely out of sight, on went the kettle and out from hiding places came the mugs, only to find the 'boss' sometimes reappearing around the other corner to catch everyone red handed!

Before the war this was the one Department that relied almost totally on casual labour. In line with building trade practice, men were laid off after 11 months to avoid the expense of holidays and superannuation. Even so, the Co-op men benefited from some excellent training and always enjoyed Union rates of pay. Some brilliant careers were shaped in the Co-op Works Dept., for one or two former apprentices eventually ended up with successful businesses of their own.

During 40 years' service as an Electrician, Ben Smelt worked in virtually every branch and department and became one of the Society's best-known figures. As a member of the CRS Regional Committee, Ben's intimate knowledge of its buildings and operations still comes in useful today. While an indentured apprentice, one of his first tasks was to work on an important contract to instal lighting in public air raid shelters around the city. He ruefully recollects having to drill hundreds of holes in solid concrete walls, all entirely by hand! House wiring was also tackled, a typical installation comprising seven lights and a plug for £7. In later years an unusual assignment was rigging up the Christmas lighting display on the exterior of the Jameson Street Store. The job entailed erecting ten 6' tall decorative stars, dressing 17 Christmas trees and hanging precariously over the edge of the massive building to position 20 coloured lighting strips. More than 2,000 lamps

All in a day's work: A Traffic Department gang prepare to tow a fire-damaged mobile shop from Bilton Grange to Holmes Street (Picture by courtesy of Mr. H. Plaxton).

A busy scene in the Joinery Workshop at Fern Street. On the left is the Foreman Mr. W.E. Owst. Also shown are: Herbert Kilvington, Wm. Webster, Walter Daddy, Herbert Gaze, Fred Jordan and W.B. Withers (Picture by courtesy of Mr. C.E. Collinson).

were used, with a total power consumption of some 30 Kilowatts every hour.

It fell to a new Works Manager, Mr. Broughton, to organise a massive post-war reconstruction programme, which kept the Department exceptionally busy until well into the 1950s. At its peak around 50 workmen were employed in all trades, the number fluctuating with the workload. Maimed shop fronts, roofs and gutters badly needed restoring and in 1947 a team of refrigeration engineers was set on to instal 'fridges in every Grocery store.

The final new construction project was the Funeral Home on Holderness Road in 1963/4. Thanks to the bricklaying prowess of men like Jack Ebbatson (who had honed his skills on the brick-lined blast furnaces at Scunthorpe Steelworks) and Ken Conland, the job was finished in double-quick time, the Manager's flat taking a mere seven days to build. However, changing economics eventually led to a concentration on 'care and maintenance' work, the Department joining Traffic at Ryde Avenue until CRS finally closed it down in 1981.

DRUG, PHARMACY AND OPTICAL DEPARTMENTS

Superintendent Chemists:	Superintendent Opticians:
L.J. Keen MPS MICO	L.J. Keen MPS MICO
F.F. Stevenson MPS FSMC	F. Howie FBOA
R. Crapper MPS FSMC	J. Laycock MPS FBOA
R.W. Simmonds MPS	D.H. Barfour-Awuah FSMC
S. Cooper MPS	J. Slater BSc. FBOA FSMC
P. McCree MPS	
D. Hutton MPS	

Branches (* Drugs only):

Jameson Street	1928-1941	1947-1982
373 Hessle Road	1930-1967	
Beverley, 44 Toll Gavel	*1944-1967	
275 Anlaby Road	*1945-1967	
Bridlington, 32 King Street	*1947-1967	
Hessle, Gisburn Road	*1954-1965	
Greenwich Avenue	1955-1976	

Drug Warehouses:

Osborne Street	1935-1941
Coltman Street	1941-1944
592 Hessle Road	1944-1955
Canning Street	1955-1969

The Hull Co-op had always sold over-the-counter drugs and remedies in its Grocery branches but the services of a dispensing chemist and an ophthalmic optician were not provided until 1928. The new Department was based at Jameson Street, with a branch at Rugby Street, and once a fortnight the optician paid a visit to members in the Bridlington area.

To comply with the law and with Pharmaceutical Society regulations, a separate subsidiary society - HULL CO-OPERATIVE CHEMISTS LTD. - was registered on 30th November 1944. Its Board comprised that of the parent Society together with the Superintendent Chemist, who by law was required to be a Director.

Two more drug businesses were acquired in the 1940s: Mr. Jas. Fraser's of Anlaby Road and Mr. Wm. Mason's of Beverley. Mr. Mason's property in Toll Gavel turned out to be steeped in history, for a secret basement was discovered containing bayonets believed to date back to the Napoleonic wars; the unusual cast-iron snakes entwining the door pillars were also quite a talking point in the ancient market town. A shortage of qualified pharmacists frustrated the original plans to develop these outlets into full chemist's shops. More successful in this regard was the Greenwich Avenue Pharmacy, which served Hull's then largest Corporation housing estate most usefully for 21 years.

Labelling medicines, counting out and bottling pills, and weighing and packing powders such as bicarbonate of soda were all part of the daily round for the four men and three girls employed at Dairycoates Drug Warehouse. It was situated over the old Co-op Stables and huge 50 gallon drums of CWS Cough Mixture and Glycerine had to be hoisted up on chains before being poured out into the bottling machines. The branches sent in their orders every Monday morning and when the staff had boxed up their requirements they took turns to accompany the van driver from Traffic on his rounds. Rita Border has good reason to recall this particular duty, for hers was one of many marriages forged through the Co-op. Her future husband, Bob, happened to be the Department's regular driver!

Under the 1960s modernisation programme, the Drug stores enjoyed a new lease of life as Wine shops. The Central Pharmacy continued trading until the Jameson Street Store closed in 1982.

The Society's Optical Department was well respected locally. A mainstay of the practice was Miss Edna Capes, the Senior Receptionist and Dispensing Assistant. Miss Capes spent her entire working life there and was popular with clients and colleagues alike. To gain the benefits of belonging to a national chain, the practice was transferred to the CWS on 13th September 1977. Co-op Eye Care still operates most successfully on that basis from King Edward Street in the city centre.

OTHER DEPARTMENTS

Wawne, Kenley House Farm (412 acres)	1916-1943
Weel, Ferry Farm (66 acres)	1917-1930
Dunswell, Dringhouses Farm (118 acres)	1921-1946
Park Avenue, Nursery Gardens	1920-1930
Withernsea, Queen Street (Cafe)	1915-1931
Bridlington, Manor Street (Cafe)	1916-1931
Jameson Street (Arcade Cafe)	1923-1941
Jameson Street (Skyline Restaurant/Ballroom)	1962-1971
Jameson Street (Coffee Lounge)	1963-1982
Market Weighton, High Street (Skyline Grill)	1964- ?
Primrose Valley, Filey (Southcliffe Hotel)	1964-1969
344 Holderness Road (Holderness Garage)	1952-1970
Anlaby High Road (Trenton Service Station)	1967-1980
Southcoates Lane (Southcoates Service Station)	1964-1966
Boothferry Road (Boothferry Car Sales)	1968-1976

The Society went in for farming primarily to support its Dairy operation but the other possibilities were quickly appreciated. Cattle and pigs could be transferred into the Slaughterhouse; hay and straw supplied to the Stables; eggs, potatoes and orchard fruit to the Grocery. All this was in line with the ambition of Co-operators to bring the production of as many commodities as possible - from farm to table - under their direct control.

Unfortunately it entered agriculture when the industry was at a low ebb and the farms ran up heavy financial losses. Faced with the troubles encountered in 1919/20 some farmers might easily have contemplated suicide: The turnip crop was wiped out by wire worm; thirty calves succumbed to a serious disease; many of the pigs died from Tuberculosis; and bad weather prevented several fields being brought into production.

By 1927 the farms' losses were having such an impact on the already depressed dividend rate that a Members' Meeting instructed Management to sell them forthwith. But, as so often happens, the resolution proved far easier to pass than to implement. Despite numerous attempts to negotiate their disposal, not until 1946 did the Society manage to extricate itself completely from what had turned out to be a costly failure.

Another venture that failed to live up to its original expectations was Catering. On 30th November 1962 a Gala Dance featuring Humphrey Lyttleton and his Orchestra launched the Skyline Restaurant and Ballroom, a massive leisure suite on the fourth floor of the new Jameson Street Store. The complex comprised a Ballroom (with resident orchestra) capable of dining 550 guests, a Café de Paris for parties of 200, a German-style Beergarden with revolving dance floor, and three smaller function rooms.

During the 'swinging sixties' the Skyline attracted many of the top flight bands of the day and hosted some of the most prestigious events in Hull's social calendar. It was a premier venue for boxing tournaments, fashion shows,

Rita Ingram (now Border) and Val Eves (now Kirman) of the Dairycoates Drug Warehouse with the handcart they shared with the Grocery branch. Note the top rail over which a tarpaulin cover was draped during inclement weather (Picture by courtesy of Mrs R. Border).

Loading milk churns at Kenley House Farm. Although the Hull Co-op failed to make a success of farming, the CWS is today Britain's biggest farmer, with 80,000 acres under its management.

Arcade Cafe, Jameson Street. After a long wait in the dividend queue, many a weary housewife would treat herself to tea and a fresh cream cake here until the Luftwaffe put paid to such little pleasures one night in 1941.

Workmen from J.A. Hewitson's laying the sprung maplewood dance floor during construction of the Skyline Ballroom, March 1962 (Picture by courtesy of Innes Studios).

Dancing contests were often staged in the Skyline Ballroom, a focal point of Hull's social life in the 1960s.

exhibitions and business gatherings of all kinds. Yet, despite an impressive client list it was every bit as unprofitable as the farms had been 40 years earlier. Perhaps it had arrived on the scene a little too late; the era of the spacious ballroom was rapidly becoming eclipsed by that of the more intimate discotheque. In 1971 the Directors conceded defeat and leased the Skyline to the Bailey Organisation for conversion into a night club.

Widening car ownership in the 1960s encouraged the Directors to regard motor trading as another business of the future. The Society operated a trio of petrol filling stations and started to sell cars, with franchises for the Volvo marque at Boothferry and Renault at Trenton. Some success was undoubtedly enjoyed for a time but it gradually became clear that the venture needed more capital and managerial time than the Society could spare, given the pressures on its mainstream business. A phased withdrawal was therefore completed by October 1980.

APPENDIX C: EMPLOYEES' RECREATION AND WELFARE

Recreation Grounds:

Cottingham Road	1926-1927
Endike Lane	1927-1932
Oak Road	1932-1978

Co-operative societies have always endeavoured to provide exemplary working conditions for their staff; the Hull Society was no exception. Its leading role in granting half-day breaks and honouring Trade Union negotiated pay and benefits has already been noted. Similarly, pensions, paid holidays, sick pay, training and welfare were all areas where the Co-op was believed to be ahead of the field or at least on a par with the best. 'Everyone was envious if they heard you had a job at the Co-op,' one former shop worker remarked. 'It was regarded as the best paid job in town, especially for a woman. We were on nearly the same money as the men, 20 years before Equal Pay became law.' Such sentiments no doubt help to explain why so many employees spent their entire working life with the Society.

Equal concern was shown for the workers in their off-duty hours, for in 1925 an EMPLOYEES' RECREATION, SOCIAL AND WELFARE CLUB was formed. It was run by an enthusiastic Committee of employees and funded by a penny a week deduction from wages.

A Sports Field was opened on Cottingham Road and a Mr. Jordan appointed as Groundsman. Perhaps there were more spectators than players at first, for one of his specified duties was 'to encourage all employees visiting the Field to take part in some game or other before leaving'. After two 'evictions' to make way for building developments, the Club finally settled at Oak Road, where a splendid 15-acre Recreation Ground was officially opened by Councillor Isaac Robinson on 21st July 1932. With all the usual match pitches, nine tennis courts and a bowling green, it was arguably one of the finest sports grounds in Hull.

Sub-Committees were set up to organise each pastime; initially these comprised Thursday Cricket, Thursday and Saturday Football, Tennis, Bowls, Swimming, Whist and Entertainments. Netball, Billiards, Cycling and Rifle Shooting were soon added to the list and there was even a flourishing Chrysanthemum Club with its own Annual Show. Until Sunday sport became acceptable after the last war, however, shop workers had to align fixtures to the half-day holiday observed by their particular department. Thus, with more than 30 teams to play in Hull's Thursday Soccer League, Thursdays were every bit as busy as Saturdays on the Co-op Field.

Indoor activities - Whist Drives in the Arcade Café and 'Rec. Club' Dances and Prize Giving

Besides the Society Trip, some Departments organised their own staff outings. A number of colleagues from Jameson Street have joined in this 1950s Works Department excursion, about to depart from Ferensway (Picture by courtesy of Mr. B. Smelt).

Former Co-op employees still have fond recollections of well-supported Gala Days at Oak Road.

The Hull Co-operative Rugby Team showing off their trophies at the end of the 1954-5 season (Picture by courtesy of Mrs R. Border).

Concerts at Beverley Road Baths - also attracted mass support. But the event most often recalled whenever old colleagues come together is the Annual Trip. With most branches closed for a full day instead of the customary afternoon, it was the one event of the year capable of bringing the Society to a virtual standstill. The excursion platforms at Paragon Station were buzzing with excitement as more than 2,000 employees and their families thronged on to special trains bound for Scarborough, Blackpool or Skegness. The Board granted each worker £1 towards their train fare and spending money, which at one time was ample to treat the whole family to a thoroughly good day out. Scarborough was invariably the favourite destination; being the shorter (and therefore cheaper) journey, new members quickly cottoned on to the fact that they would have more pocket money left!

In 1951 the Club, for some obscure reason, voted to deviate from normal practice and travel by motor coach. Some fifty-four coaches, the largest fleet ever to set off from Ferensway, had to be drafted in from far and wide for the event. Crossing the Yorkshire Wolds en route to the coast, the snake-like procession must have caused some looks of astonishment in the villages along the way! Happily, the day proceeded without a hitch but afterwards the Police probably had something to say about the traffic congestion, for no mass excursion by road was ever attempted again.

The final Trip ran in 1967 but the tradition of closing the shops had vanished 14 years earlier when, to avoid upsetting shoppers, it was switched to a Sunday or Bank Holiday Monday.

As time went by the Oak Road pitches were being hired out more often than the staff teams were using them. Like others, the Co-op Ground had fallen victim to the post-war decline in works-based sport. After its closure in 1978 it was sad to see the once lovingly-tended sward lying deserted and overgrown.

The Club's achievements over its 60-year life reflect the hard work of many dedicated supporters. People like Johnny Burns, its Secretary 1928-47; George Bayes, a keen Rugby League man (likewise 1950-75); Walter Kirk, a respected Honorary President; Bill Oxley, its long-serving Treasurer; Bill's wife Jean; and Samuel Marshall, whose tireless efforts helped to get it started. Not forgetting countless Committee members, each of whom in their day contributed to its success.

Two other staff-based ventures also deserve mentioning: The HULL CO-OPERATIVE MUTUAL AID ASSOCIATION (1928-60) helped employees to get by when they fell on hard times. It too was funded by regular stoppages from pay. Then, in 1970 the HULL CO-OPERATIVE RETIRED EMPLOYEES' ASSOCIATION was formed, with Fred Cant as Chairman and Bill Oxley as Secretary. The 'Co-op Pensioners' still look forward to their monthly get-togethers when they can catch up on Society developments and hear news of colleagues they have known. The meetings have a wider therapeutic value of course and many humorous tales, gathered up over a lifetime's service, are swapped with old friends time and again without losing any of their original flavour! If this book rekindles a few more memories of those 'good old days' then it will not have been written in vain.

APPENDIX D: 'TO MAKE A BETTER WORLD'

CO-OPERATIVE EDUCATION

Educational Secretaries:

Thos. Penn
Walter Horton
W.H. Bailey
John H. Scarlett
Walter Litchfield
R. Robinson
John P. Prince
Mrs H. Fenwick

Wm. H. Saunders
James R. Glasby
Mrs G. Brown
Mrs Kathleen Overton
George S. Burton
Mrs Lilian Goring

Member Relations Secretaries:

Mrs Joan Broadwell
George S. Burton
John E. Smith

Co-operative Institutes/Halls:

Jarratt Street   1902-1904
30 Albion Street   1904-1931
Kingston Square   1931-1974
77-9 Charles Street 1975-1983

Unity Halls/Guildrooms:

Holland Street
Dairycoates
Bridlington, Quay Road
Derby Street
Howden, Churchside
Marfleet
Withernsea, Queen Street
Cottingham, Hallgate
Hornsea, Newbegin
Beverley, Beaver Road
Hessle, Grovehill.

The Hull Society was as keen as any to cultivate well-informed members, interested in helping it to progress. The Rules permitted up to 2½% of the profits to be devoted to this work, which was organised by an elected Educational Committee. The Committee's declared aim was to enable everyone, should they so desire, to 'place the Co-op at the very heart of their existence'. They would be able to shop in a Co-operative store, attend a Co-operative lecture or concert, learn at a Co-operative school, enjoy a Co-operative excursion and even read a Co-operative newspaper.

A Reading Room was provided in Jarratt Street where members could go to study, or have read to them, books and periodicals of every kind.

The Committee ran classes; laid on talks, socials and magic lantern shows; sponsored choirs and a String Band; and even staged an Annual Flower Show. Scholarships were awarded to Co-op Union Summer Schools, for which members had to write a 1,000 word essay. And by 1912 Saturday night lecture-concerts featuring Casey and his Fiddle were regularly taking place at that pinnacle of the city's cultural life - the Royal Institution in Albion Street. The Committee evidently considered no venue too grand for the Co-operators of Hull.

To convert shoppers into members, and members into active Co-operators, PROPAGANDA CONCERTS were staged in all parts of the Society's vast trading area. Before the television age people thought nothing of walking three or four miles, in all weathers, to attend such an event. A clever blend of propaganda and entertainment, the format enabled the case for Co-operation to be punched home with gusto. Mr. Marshall, the General Manager, was often present to speak with pride of his Society's healthy Balance Sheet and generous dividend rate. Then there would be a rousing speech from a Committee member, many of whom were gifted orators, skilled at putting a Co-operative slant on any topic of the day. Once the audience had been inspired, the refreshments consumed, the concert applauded and the membership forms gathered in, everyone would set off for home clutching their free sample of Lutona Cocoa or Crumpsall Biscuits.

The Co-op made imaginative use of film in its propaganda work, the CWS Talkie Film Unit making week-long tours of East Yorkshire. *The Cup that Cheers* was a movie describing the production of Co-op Tea; *A Matter of Form* dealt tastefully with CWS Desbeau Corsets, while *Bubbles* promoted CWS Soap. There were educational newsreels too, and historical documentaries such as *The Men of Rochdale*, produced for the 1944 Centenary.

The Committee's most onerous responsibility was to provide CLASSES for employees and members. As the Hull Municipal Technical College's largest 'customer' the Society was allowed to turn the Osborne Street School into a 'Co-op College' three nights a week, with its own teachers. During its mid-1930s heyday more than 1,000 students attended lectures there every week in subjects ranging from Co-operative Book-keeping, Co-operation and Citizenship, Shop Practice and Commodities to English, Commercial Arithmetic and Branch Organisation. Art, Drama, Literature, Singing, Elocution, Public Speaking and Dressmaking were also taught, plus special courses for women and children, tutored by leading members of the Women's Guild.

At the end of term, students would sit for exams set by the Co-operative Union; for an employee, a Co-op Union Certificate or Diploma was a coveted passport to promotion. At the prize-giving ceremony which followed, one or two scholarships might also be handed out, offering some promising working-class boy or girl the chance of a lifetime - to continue their education at a nationally-renowned seat of learning. The Committee took the supervision of *their college* very seriously, firmly believing that helping people from modest backgrounds to acquire a zest for learning would lead them on to a richer, more purposeful life. As one-time student Doug Widdowson put it: 'The classes gave us youngsters a great enthusiasm for the ideals of the Co-operative Movement. It spurred us on to know we were not just in the business of selling food or furniture; we were helping to build a better, more just world.'

In the 1950s the numbers passing through never again reached pre-war proportions. After the Butler educational reforms, bright scholars who might have taken a job at the Co-op on leaving school at 14 or 15 were increasingly 'lost' to the Grammar Schools. The non-vocational classes, now largely duplicated by local authority provision, were abandoned in 1951. By 1970 new legislation had ushered in a different approach to staff development; as a result the Educational Committee relinquished its duties to a full-time Staff Training Officer.

Distributing CO-OPERATIVE LITERATURE was another high priority. An ardent Co-operator once had an astonishing choice of reading matter. From your Grocery branch you could order *Co-operative News* (1d. weekly); *Women's Outlook* (1d. fortnightly); *Our Circle* (1d. monthly, for children); *Producer* (3d. monthly), and *Millgate Monthly* (6d.). Yet another topical magazine was *The Wheatsheaf* (later renamed *Home*), nationally-produced but with up to four pages of Hull Society news. And in a Co-operative home no weekend was complete without a thorough perusal of *Reynold's News* - the only Co-operatively-owned Sunday newspaper.

Taking advantage of group travel discounts, the Committee became expert at organising EXCURSIONS on a grand scale. In an era when few industrial workers enjoyed paid holidays, and many rarely travelled anywhere, they would charter a train from the LNER and whisk 400 members away to some far-off beauty spot. It must have posed a formidable challenge, however, to make sure everyone boarded the right trains or boats, and got home exactly as planned. The 1935 tour, for instance, involved a steamer trip along the North Wales coast, free time in Llandudno, an evening in Southport, and three meals en route! The fare? Just 27/6d. (£1.37). The one in 1939 (the last in peace time) was reportedly the finest ever, taking in Stratford-on-Avon and the Severn Valley, and partaking of fresh Ross-on-Wye Salmon for tea - one of four good meals for an all-inclusive 32/6d. (£1.63).

The name of John P. Prince was synonymous with Co-op Education throughout the 1930s. A flamboyant character, he was a Grocery Branch Manager by trade but most of his spare time and energy was devoted to the cause - as

Educational Secretary, class tutor and editor of the local pages of *The Wheatsheaf*. Jack is also credited with forming the Good Companions' Motor Club, a group of Co-operatively-connected car and motorbike enthusiasts who enjoyed regular Sunday trips into the countryside until petrol rationing put paid to their hobby.

In the 'thirties, when a whole generation seemed in danger of drifting into what were termed 'organisations of a really militant character', Co-op YOUTH WORK - with its emphasis on peaceful values - was like a breath of fresh air. It was organised into three stages: Playways classes for 7 to 11 year olds; Pathfinder groups for 11s to 14s; Youth Clubs and Woodcraft Folk Fellowships for over 14s. The teenage members (some of whom were lucky enough to have a foothold on the Co-op career ladder) camped at Drewton Dale, enjoyed dances and talks, and met at Cecil Corner for Sunday hikes to Beverley Westwood or Paull Foreshore. It was only a matter of time before a handful of marriages ensued! A couple of Co-op employees, Robin Kerridge and Tony Rippon, again took up the challenge of opening a Co-op Youth Club in the 'sixties when young people faced many new pressures. With its own little candlelit coffee bar tucked away from the outside world, the Club did a lot of good work.

The 1944 Centennial Pageant - itself a wonderful example of practical Co-operation - revived interest in the performing arts. According to former Educational Secretary Lilian Goring: 'New friendships were formed, and a number of drama groups sprang up in the Women's Guilds; in my view the quality of their output compared favourably with many a semi-professional show.' Then, in the 1950s, James and Lucie Glasby formed the UNITY PLAYERS, whose creative talents came together to present up to four plays a year before capacity audiences at the Institute. Also around this time, Charles Thompson (soon to become the Society's Chief Cashier) was directing three

CO-OPERATIVE CHOIRS (Ladies', Girls' and Junior) accompanied by his colleague Tom Medd. Encouraged by these gifted gentlemen the choirs enjoyed a distinguished record in competition and, for more than 30 years, brought immense pleasure to countless audiences.

Bill Saunders, a senior clerk at the CWS Flour Mills, was Educational Secretary through the 1950s. Meetings, debates, conferences, At Homes and day schools all formed part of the staple fare as his Committee strove to quench a seemingly insatiable thirst for knowledge among Hull Co-op members. Even the employees were happy to spend their Saturday half-holiday listening to a good visiting lecturer. WEEKEND SCHOOLS, often at the Majestic Hotel, Scarborough, are still fondly remembered by those active in the Society at the time, though one suspects as much for the lively social side as the lecture content, despite such erudite contributors as Hull's own Jim Peddie. And visits to Co-op factories crept into the itinerary for members' trips: More than 100 went to the Crumpsall Biscuit works; 250 toured Middleton Preserves; 75 visited Worksop Glass; two coachloads inspected the CWS Hosiery works at Huthwaite.

Looking back, the educational work of the 1950s and 1960s had a distinctly international dimension. When talks on the work of the United Nations revealed the plight of the emerging nations of Africa and Asia, members resolved, in true Co-operative spirit, to offer practical help by sponsoring the education of two boys, one from the Lebanon and one from Uganda. And a HULL CO-OPERATIVE ESPERANTO ASSOCIATION was formed; before long some four dozen enthusiasts were gathering weekly to forge overseas links in this unique transnational language.

Sponsoring clubs and groups figured prominently in the Committee's work. Foremost among these was the HULL CO-OPERATIVE

MEMBERS' OVER SIXTIES ASSOCIATION which Albert Fergusson and Fred Magson founded in 1958. With 640 members on its books it was soon acknowledged as one of the biggest pensioners' clubs in the country. Members met in the Institute every Wednesday to enjoy talks, concerts, old time dancing, whist and dominoes - plus a refreshing cup of Co-op 99 Tea. Seven coaches were needed for the annual summer trip which even merited a civic send-off by the Lord Mayor. Panto' visits were arranged, funds raised to train Guide Dogs for the Blind and in countless other ways the Club brightened up the lives of folk who might otherwise have been destined to sit at home, with only a radio for company.

When the new Co-operative Hall opened in 1975 it provided a base for an amazing range of activities: Dancing and Keep Fit Classes; Over 60s, Gardening, Camera and Luncheon Clubs; Choirs; Retired Employees' and Branch Managers' Associations; the Ventura Players Drama Group and three branches of the Women's Guild.

By now the Educational Committee had been superseded by a MEMBER RELATIONS COMMITTEE, challenged with giving Co-op Education a more modern look. As this Committee's Secretary, the writer was privileged to play a small part in the task. It worked with schools and like-minded community groups to promote Co-operative values and sponsored a host of novel ventures, raising thousands of pounds to buy equipment for the local hospitals in the process. Although, sadly, the Co-operative Hall has since gone (the building is now the New Clarence public house), the CRS Humberside Member Relations Committee continues to put on a lively programme of events for Co-op members, often centred on the Society's own stores.

CO-OPERATIVE GUILDS

From humble Yorkshire origins in 1883, the CO-OPERATIVE WOMEN'S GUILD grew into a national force dedicated to promoting Co-operative values and the welfare of the people. Hull's first branch - Central - opened on 25th June 1895; others quickly followed in East, West and North Hull.

The West Hull Guild's first minute book, recently lent to the writer, faithfully records those early days when 14 women had scrambled into an attic over Featherstone's Eating House at 329 Hessle Road. Within two years of the inaugural meeting on 4th December 1901, the numbers had grown to 60 and members were looking forward to having their own permanent Guild Room over a brand-new Co-op shop at Dairycoates.

Every Tuesday night, ordinary women from the back streets of West Hull would put aside their household chores and gather to enjoy the comradeship of their Guild, listen to talks and debate the burning topics of the day. Topics like Home Nursing; Co-operation in poor neighbourhoods; the Ideals of a Prison Visitor; Educating the young according to Robert Owen; Public health; The care of feeble-minded children; Co-operative banking; Leadless glass; Child slaves; and Co-operative garden cities.

Women's Suffrage naturally had its place on the agenda and even in those days there was interest in 'Vegetarian food and its uses'. Being hard-working folk whose hands were unaccustomed to idleness, members would often bring their sewing along to meetings. Yet it wasn't all sober business and dry as dust debates - far from it! The syllabus was liberally sprinkled with concerts, dances, Strawberry Teas and socials, when the Guildswomen would let their hair down, have a bit of fun and perhaps raise a few coppers for the Poor Bairns Boot Fund.

A wagonette ride to North Ferriby or West Ella passed a pleasant summer evening; on the way a call was invariably made at the Sculcoates

Union Cottage Homes to treat the orphan children to a rare trip into the country. 'Brakes for 40 were supplied by Mr. Hudson of Anlaby Road at a charge of 9d. each,' the Minute Book carefully records.

Much of the Guild's work in fact revolved around children. There were Junior Classes to inspire them with Co-operative History and Principles, and over 150 would sit down to tea with their mothers for the annual Christmas Treat.

Officers of the Guild branches devoted hours to recruiting new members, sometimes commandeering a chair in the local Co-op from which to approach female customers as they shopped. Another method was doorstep canvassing. Soon after setting up home on the new Bilton Grange estate, Nellie Senior received a visitation from two formidable women dressed in furs and big hats. 'I'd like to join,' she began in response to their persuasive tones, 'but as you can see I'm expecting.' 'Oh don't worry about that, love, bring your baby with you,' they replied. Nellie did just that, remaining a member for over 40 years.

Once recruited, enthusiasm for Guild work knew no bounds; only illness or a death in the family kept members away. As one-time East Hull member Emily Hodgson pointed out, in busy households where the menfolk were involved in, say, Friendly Society or Trade Union work, it was firmly understood that Father must stay in to look after the children on Mother's Guild night.

With their forthright views on how society ought to be organised, the Guilds naturally gravitated towards politics. Jane Humber of the *Hull Daily Mail* credited them with teaching women 'to think and stand up for themselves, to fight for benefits, divorce and education reforms, insurance for women and of course the vote'. Campaigns were staged for women police, a minimum wage, family allowances, prison reform, advice on contraceptives and better maternity care, to name but a few.

In 1929 a Hull Guildswoman was elected as a Co-operative/Labour City Councillor. During her 12-years service Cllr. Mrs Lilian Alderson tirelessly pushed forward the social reforms that had been hammered out year after year in the city's Guild rooms. In poorer areas like the one she represented, the mortality rates for mothers and infants were appalling. She pressed for ante-natal care and in 1936 the North Hull Municipal Clinic, the first of its kind in the country, was opened. Similarly, Mrs Alderson's campaigning for better child care facilities bore fruit when she laid the foundation stone of the McMillan Nursery, Hull's first purpose-built nursery school.

By 1950 the 19 Guild branches attached to the Hull Co-operative Society were exerting a powerful influence on its affairs, acting almost as a natural counterbalance to that of its employees. Guildswomen were studious attenders at Members' Meetings, keen to exercise their right to vote and keep Management on their toes with some well-aimed questions. They themselves were an important source of Educational Committee members and Directors, with no fewer than a dozen of their number gracing the Hull Society's Board room during the post-war era.

For its members the Guild brought new friendships and the chance to do things they had scarcely dreamed of. Like many, Flo Smith was gradually drawn into its work after a neighbour invited her to join the Hessle Branch: 'Standing up for the first time to give the greetings at another Guild's Birthday Tea was a shattering experience,' she admitted, 'but as time went by I gained more confidence in myself and learnt more and more about things outside the home. The Guild gave me a whole new outlook on life.'

Visiting other Guilds to take part in 'Any Questions' panels; singing Guild songs;

Co-op evening classes met in the Board Room at Jarratt Street after the Osborne Street Centre was bombed (Picture by courtesy of Mr. E. Williamson).

Co-operative Youth Club outing to Sledmere in 1945. The Club's Leaders - Emily and Cyril Hodgson - contributed much to the Society's social life for nearly half a century.

The cast and back-stage staff of Great Day, a Unity Players production of the 1960s. After playing to capacity audiences at the Institute the play went 'on tour' to the local hospitals (Picture by courtesy of Mrs Joyce Cook).

The Co-operative Singers with their accompanist Tom Medd (left) and conductor Charles Thompson. The Singers raised valuable funds for causes such as the Multiple Sclerosis Society. They also cut two LP records, the last one - Thirty Years of Song - marking an important anniversary in 1980.

Hull and East Riding Co-op members at the birthplace of the Co-operative Movement - the tiny store in Toad Lane, Rochdale - in 1979, shortly after it reopened as a Museum.

The Co-operative Pipe Band leading the 1980 International Co-operators' Day Parade from the Jameson Street Store to the Co-op Hall (Picture by courtesy of Mr. David Morrison)

performing in Concert Parties; parading proudly behind their elaborately-decorated Guild banners; and attending International Day fetes are among the cherished memories of Guild activists. And once a year most branches would host a Birthday Tea and an At Home.

One of Clarice Scruton's first tasks, on joining in the 1940s, was to help clear up the bombed North Hull Guild Room in Derby Street. Clarice went on to hold office at Branch, District and Section level and in 1966 was chosen to go to Vienna for the International Co-operative Alliance Congress: 'It was a very emotional experience, with delegates in national costume from Russia, Poland, Germany and so on, all pledging themselves for World Peace.' In 1994, soon after stepping down as President of the Newland Guild, Clarice celebrated her 100th birthday. Her friends honoured her with a special luncheon at the University of Hull at which the Lord Mayor and the Chairman of CRS paid tribute to her long service to her home city and the Co-operative Movement.

The emphasis at Guild meetings gradually shifted from formal lectures to open discussions, Brains Trusts, quizzes, games nights, outings and fund-raising for national and local causes. The aim of these subtle changes was to attract the younger, better educated woman. But it was an uphill task when so many were embarking on careers that left them little spare time for meetings. Perhaps the Guild had become a victim of its own success. There again, at least one member thought it a sad commentary on modern society that some women would rather spend their leisure hours playing 'mindless games of Bingo' than extending their knowledge. And even sadder, when they had cause to feel nervous about walking out to meetings after dark.

All these factors affected Guild membership and, one by one, branches faded away until in 1998 only one remains in Hull, meeting on Monday afternoons at the Railway Institute in the city centre. Some of the more strident campaigning of yesteryear may have receded into the background as the hard-fought-for social reforms have steadily been won, but the Guild can still offer stimulating activities and companionship to those joining its ranks.

The HULL CO-OPERATIVE MEN'S GUILD began in 1928 and met weekly in the Institute for nearly 40 years. Branches were also founded at Marfleet, Beverley and Hessle. Though having similar aspirations, the Men's Guilds never attracted the wide following that the Women's Guilds did. But they had their own motto - Unrestricted Co-operation for All Purposes of Life - and ran their own insurance schemes. The CMG was superseded by the NATIONAL GUILD OF CO-OPERATORS, a mixed guild of men and women which continued to meet in Hull until about 1980.

A VOICE IN GOVERNMENT

Though the Rochdale Pioneers believed that strict political neutrality offered the best way of attaining their ultimate goal of a Co-operative Commonwealth, Co-operators have never been afraid to campaign for changes that would give ordinary people a fairer chance in life. However, during the First World War big business interests, which were well represented in Parliament, conspired to push the Co-op well down the queue for essential food supplies and thwart its progress in various other ways. To protect itself, the Movement resolved in 1917 to found its own political party.

In Hull the newly-formed Co-operative Party worked alongside the Trades Council and Labour Party to get Co-operators elected to the City Council and other public bodies. Its first of many successes came in February 1920 when Walter Litchfield swept to victory in Myton Ward by a majority of two to one. Apparently the Co-op's landaulette proved a great asset in his campaign!

Guild branches often had concert parties in which members practised their dramatic talents. Here we see East Hull CWG's Kitchenette Band. The melodious singing of the Guildswomen could be heard in Woolworth's stock room across the road.

Members of the Newland Co-operative Women's Guild in 1977.

The Lord Mayor and Lady Mayoress of Kingston upon Hull, Councillor and Mrs H. Woodford, congratulate members of the Women's Guild on the occasion of the Guild Movement's centenary in 1983. Receiving the bouquet are Mrs N. Senior and Mrs L. Wallis, the Yorkshire District Secretary and President.

Eighty years later the Party is still a vigorous force in local politics, with seven of Hull's 60 City Councillors designated 'Labour and Co-operative' as well as several members of the East Riding of Yorkshire Council. Hosting the National Co-operative Party Conference over the 1991 Easter Weekend was a recent highspot for local Party members. More than 600 delegates and guests converged on Hull City Hall - many of them visiting the city for the first time - to receive a real Yorkshire welcome. A rousing address by the then Shadow Cabinet Member John Prescott MP launched the event in a truly memorable way.

APPENDIX E: SOME OTHER CO-OPERATIVES IN EAST YORKSHIRE

BEVERLEY AND DISTRICT CO-OPERATIVE SOCIETY LIMITED

With its shipyard and tannery, Beverley was an important industrial centre in the late 19th century. A Co-operative Society was formed there on 2nd March 1899, at a meeting in the Baptist Schoolroom presided over by a Mr. C.J. Gill. When members' subscriptions reached £25 an account was opened with the Beverley Savings Bank and four members went out in search of a shop.

In 1915 the Society was based at 25-31 Eastgate; it had 675 members and paid a divi of 1/4d. in the £. A branch was about to open in Grovehill Road. Six years later a separate Drapery Store was opened on the corner of Wednesday Market and Railway Street; as with the Grocery, this later moved into Toll Gavel.

After a decade of flagging fortunes the 1,281-member Society agreed in 1929 to amalgamate with Hull. At the time the Committee comprised: Messrs. Willey (President), Theakston (Vice President), Wood, Lewis, Neal, Beaumont, Gilson and Scruton. The Secretary and General Manager was Mr. F. Hirst.

BRIDLINGTON AND DISTRICT CO-OPERATIVE SOCIETY LIMITED

Some years ago the writer interviewed Mrs Ethel Hamerton, the daughter of one of the pioneers, who was able to relate from memory how the Society had come about.

Mrs Hamerton's father, Mr. Alf Wiles (a master builder and joiner), often took a Sunday morning walk in Bessingby Fields with two of his pals - Mr. Patterson and Mr. Beswick. They would stroll and chat while their children played on the grass. One day the conversation turned to the 'sharp practices' that certain shopkeepers sometimes employed in order to inflate their takings. Mrs Wiles, it seems, had been treated rather rudely by her family grocer after complaining that he had re-priced a block of butter overnight. Having heard of Co-operatives starting up in other towns, the men decided to write to the CWS for advice.

As a result they subscribed £5 each to buy from the CWS as much 'Christmas cheer' as they could. The goods were re-sold from Mr. Beswick's parlour at 53 Quay Road. Soon more and more people were clamouring to join the scheme and in 1897 a Co-op Society was formed with Mr. Beswick as Secretary and Mr. Wiles as Manager.

The presence of dusty stock made living conditions unpleasant and so a house in Midway Terrace was rented and turned into a shop, opening in the evenings and on Saturday afternoons. Young Ethel would sit on the counter while her father weighed out customers' orders and her mother tended the shelves.

After a further move, into Oxford Street, the Society bought the Singer Sewing Machine shop in Quay Road and also entered the Coal trade. As they couldn't afford a coal cell, Mr. Patterson (who worked on the railway) arranged for a full coal wagon to be left in a siding for the members to empty themselves.

At the turn of the century Mr. Wiles emigrated to Africa and a Mr. Herbert Harper was put in charge. Doubtless Mr. Harper was a fine grocer but his book-keeping skills left something to be desired and the accounts got into quite a state! When he came home three years later Mr. Wiles found his little enterprise in urgent need of rebuilding.

Operating in a seaside town, the Co-op was often asked for extended credit to see the boarding house keepers through the lean winter months. Such demands proved difficult to resist and, having very limited working capital, the Society soon found itself in financial difficulties. Leading Bridlington members decided it would be best to merge with the Hull Society, which absorbed the business in January 1908.

CO-OPERATIVE BANK PLC.

From about 1918 the Hull Co-op in Jarratt Street acted as agents for what was then the Banking Department of the CWS (Manchester). The service was widely used by Trade Unions, Friendly Societies and personal customers. Then, in 1972, the Co-operative Bank opened a branch of its own at 66 King Edward Street. Such was its popularity that in 1983 a move was made to much larger premises in Alfred Gelder Street, facing Queen's Gardens.

Now 125 years old, the Co-operative Bank is one of the UK's fastest growing banks. It has a well-deserved reputation for its innovative approach to business. Among the 'firsts' it has introduced to the banking industry are free banking for all customers who remain in credit (1973), interest-bearing current accounts (1982), extended opening hours (1987) and credit cards guaranteed free for the cardholder's lifetime. Its Armchair Banking service is one of the most widely used telephone banking operations. In recent years the Bank has become famous for its ethical policy, which clearly states who it will and will not do business with.

Customers are regularly consulted as to how their money should be invested.

CO-OPERATIVE DENTAL ASSOCIATION LTD.

At one time you could even have your teeth looked after by a Co-operative Dentist. The surgery was in Jameson Street, Hull, later moving to King Edward Street until the practice disbanded in the 1970s.

CO-OPERATIVE INSURANCE SOCIETY LTD. (CIS)

For decades the Co-op Insurance Man has been a familiar visitor to thousands of East Yorkshire homes, the first local agent (Mr. S. Lamb) being appointed as long ago as November 1890. Even before that the Hull Co-operative Provident Co. had urged support for a national Co-operative insurance scheme, after several early Co-op stores were caught out by fires at their premises for which they had no insurance cover. The CIS was consequently established by the Co-operative Movement, including some of the original Rochdale Pioneers, in 1867.

After the last war more than 80 CIS agents were operating from the Hull District Office (above the Yorkshire Penny Bank in Queen Victoria Square), one of the busiest in the country. All the clients' records had been burnt during the Blitz and the local agents used their own knowledge to help piece them together again. Offices were later established at Festival House, Jameson Street (1951), Chariot Street (1964) and Bond Street (1967). These have since merged and relocated to the Conifer Rooms in Prospect Street.

The CIS enjoyed strong ties with the retail society. Whenever anyone joined the Stores a slip was sent to the CIS ensuring that an agent would soon appear on the member's doorstep ready to offer a service. And according to retired agent Mike Kemp: 'It was amazing how many agents were recruited from the local Co-op shops. Often they found being a CIS agent a better proposition - they used to say the sky was the limit as to what you could earn. Yet the new boys remained fiercely loyal to their old employer. They wouldn't hear a word said against the Hull Co-op!'

Another pensioner, Don Culpan, explained that the CIS operated differently to most insurance companies, in that the agents had to 'buy their own Book'. The CIS loaned them the money at a favourable rate, which they repaid over time. 'Basically any added value through the effort you put in was yours, and benefited you when the round was eventually sold on. In a sense it was like having your own business and so CIS agents perhaps tended to look after their customers that little bit better.'

Nowadays many agents use laptop computers in dealing with their customers' requirements - a far cry from the days when they had to cycle round their areas to get about! As a leading home and motor insurer, and provider of life assurance, investment plans and pensions, CIS is a major force in the UK financial services industry, constantly updating its products to meet customers' changing needs. True to its Co-operative principles, the Society uses all its profits solely to benefit the 3½ million families it serves - many of whom have stayed loyal from generation to generation.

CO-OPERATIVE PERMANENT BUILDING SOCIETY

As with the Bank and Insurance Society, the Hull Co-op Society acted as agents until a branch opened in Jameson Street opposite the Central Store. In 1970 the CPBS withdrew from the Co-operative Movement (though steadfastly remaining a mutual building society) and took a new name - the Nationwide.

CO-OPERATIVE WHOLESALE SOCIETY LTD. (CWS)

The early co-operative retail societies found they had neither the skill nor the buying power to get the best deal for their members. So in 1863 a group of them joined together to found the CWS. Gradually the CWS extended its operations beyond wholesaling into manufacturing, farming and importing.

From 1918 Hull was an important centre for producing CWS Flour and Preserves. The former Hurtley's Flour Mill at Wilmington on the River Hull supplied all the Co-ops in this part of the country. As the only one in the city to survive wartime bombing, it also stepped into the breach to support the private trade. When it closed under a rationalisation move in December 1967, 100 employees lost their jobs and 20 more retired.

The CWS Preserves Works in Cumberland Street were based in a building once known as Kingston Cotton Mill. This mill literally went down in history for its involvement in a 19th century court case which established the principle - familiar to budding accountants everywhere - that an auditor is expected to be 'a watchdog but not a bloodhound'. Many Hull folk still remember it as the 'Jam Factory'. Fruit for preserving was brought from Cannon Street railway station by horse-rulley and it was a favourite pastime of children in the neighbourhood to run after the cart and scoop up any that fell to the ground! Production was transferred to Middleton in Lancashire in 1932.

Other local CWS operations included a Fruit and Vegetable Depot in Osborne Street, Bacon Curing Works in Dansom Lane, Fish Depot in Strickland Street and Soft Drinks Warehouse at Hessle. A Scales Depot in Pelham Street (later Glasshouse Row) maintained all the weighing equipment used by the Co-op shops in the region.

Today the CWS is represented in the Hull area by a Co-op 'Eye Care' Optician's and eight branches of Co-op Travelcare, now a leading travel agency. Travelcare's presence in East

Yorkshire was given a welcome boost in 1998 when the well-respected local business known as Fiesta Travel joined the Group.

CREDIT UNIONS

Credit Unions are not-for-profit self-help financial co-operatives set up by groups of people who share some common bond (such as the same neighbourhood or employer). By providing a haven for members' savings and a source of cheap loans they help to keep people out of the clutches of indiscriminate money lenders charging exorbitant rates of interest.

Fledgling credit unions are currently operating in Beverley and North Hull (the HU6 postcode area) and there are groups working to establish others in various parts of the city, and among the employees of the City Council.

DRIFFIELD CO-OPERATIVE SOCIETY LIMITED

A co-operative society was founded in this bustling East Yorkshire market town in 1868. Initially bearing the rather cumbersome title of 'Driffield Working Men's Co-operative Industrial and Provident Society', it was based at 68 Middle Street South. According to a 1910 Directory, the Society traded in Grocery, Drapery, Boots, Furnishings, Coal, Hardware, Ironmongery, Tailoring, Earthenware and Flour. At one time it ran a branch store at Middleton on the Wolds.

In 1971 a Special Meeting of members unanimously approved the voluntary winding up of the Society. Its President, Councillor Arthur Leason, said it had fulfilled its purpose in the town and could no longer operate profitably. The property was bought by two local businessmen for conversion into shops and flats. On 18th May 1972, at the Society's final meeting in the Congregational Church Schoolroom, the 270 members were paid out their full share capital plus interest.

HULL BRUSHMAKERS LTD.

Few records remain of this co-partnership firm which was formed around 1905. It undertook 'general brushmaking' and had 42 members and £75 in share capital. By 1910 its registered address was at 20 Marlborough Terrace, Beverley Road. Employees worked a 50-hour week and were granted two days annual holidays. By 1914 the firm had ceased to exist.

HULL CO-OPERATIVE PEOPLE'S BANK

A local bank with an office in George Street, Hull. A devoted and long-serving Secretary was Walter Kirk (President of the Hull Co-operative Society). It was dissolved in 1974.

HULL GENERAL BUILDERS LTD.

Hull City Councillor Paddy Flanagan JP seems to have been the driving force behind this co-partnership, formed in 1898. As General Secretary of the Builders' Labourers Society, it was his passionate desire to improve the conditions of workers in the building trade.

Alterations and repairs for the Hull Co-operative Society kept the firm busy in its early years. In 1906 it was based at 30 Lockwood Street and had 146 members, £534 in share capital, reserve funds of £524, and five employees. Net profit was £103 on sales of £4,178. No records exist after 1911.

HULL PRINTERS LTD.

Founded in 1897, this was another firm with shares held by the workers. The lot of the Victorian printer and bookbinder was far from pleasant. He typically spent long hours in dingy, stuffy surroundings, received miserable pay and was never asked his opinion on any aspect of his work. The promoters were determined to change all that. Their premises were light and airy; they were the first Hull firm to cut the working week from 54 hours to 48; and they took the workers into partnership, letting them share in its success with pay bonuses and a chance to serve on the Committee of Management. But some regarded their stance as tantamount to a workers' revolution. One good lady advised her committee that 'no work must be sent to the Hull Printers because they are a set of Bolsheviks'!

Some of Hull's most prominent citizens served on the Management Committee in their day, including Alderman Francis Askew, Councillor Will Millington and Alderman Watson Boyes - familiar names to students of the city's Labour history.

Hull Printers undertook all kinds of printing, publishing and bookbinding work. An important annual contract was to produce the Telephone Directory for Hull Corporation, the only municipal telephone undertaking in Britain. In 1964 it took seven full weeks and consumed 48 tons of paper and 12 cwts. of ink to turn out the 90,000 copies required.

The firm went into liquidation in October 1975, the closure being blamed on a slump in the economy.

HUMBERSIDE CO-OPERATIVE DEVELOPMENT AGENCY

Over the past two decades East Yorkshire people have been discovering afresh that co-operatives can offer a viable alternative to public and private sector enterprises. By giving them the chance to control their working lives in a democratic way, they can provide jobs which are safer and more satisfying.

Formed in 1985, following a conference of interested individuals at the University of Hull, the Humberside CDA gives practical help to groups wishing to develop the commercial skills needed to run a workers' co-operative.

In workers' co-ops, as in other forms of Co-operation, control is based on one member, one vote. The members work in the business and also serve as the directors. Workers' co-ops in East Yorkshire carry on a wide variety of businesses. Some of the more successful include:

Spurn Pilots Ltd.

The pilots take responsibility for the safe passage and docking of the millions of tonnes of shipping which annually plies the Humber and its tributaries. The fast tides and rapidly moving sandbanks conspire to make river navigation a challenging task, best handled by pilots with local knowledge and experience.

The pilots realised that the best way to guarantee a quality service, regardless of time or tide, was to co-operate rather than compete. They approached the CDA who helped them set up their service as a co-op in 1988.

Giroscope Ltd.

Giroscope was formed in 1985 by a group of young homeless unemployed people, using a combination of loans and donations to buy and renovate their first house. From this self-help approach the idea expanded to help others solve their housing and unemployment problems. The co-op now lets about 20 houses to people otherwise excluded from the housing system - young people, single parents, those without deposits, and so on.

Giroscope has also helped other co-ops to get off the ground, including a creche, a printing co-operative, and People's Trading, a corner shop in the Hessle Road area with a commitment to healthy food - very like the original Rochdale Pioneers'. It is now renovating workshops to provide employment opportunities for other local people.

Homecare Co-operative Ltd.

Homecare provides care to elderly people, and people with disabilities, in their own homes.

The services vary from light assistance - cleaning and shopping - to a high level of personal care, requiring skill, sensitivity and respect for the most vulnerable members of the community.

Starting in 1993 with three members and a small amount of personal savings, Homecare has rapidly grown into a substantial service with over 100 care workers. In the best traditions of Co-operation it has managed to provide a quality service, cheaper than other care providers, while guaranteeing its members higher earnings in an industry characterised by low pay.

MARKET WEIGHTON AND DISTRICT CO-OPERATIVE SOCIETY LTD.

Established in 1903, this Society developed Grocery, Drapery, Hardware, Boots and Furniture stores in York Road and High Street, Market Weighton. It had a Butcher's shop and a Café in the town and Grocery branches at Holme-upon-Spalding-Moor, Seaton Ross and North Newbald.

In March 1963 weekly sales averaged £5,210 and the 2,334 members held £106,397 in Share Capital. Dividend was 4d. in the £ and the Directors were contemplating building a new Furnishing store on the site of the former Central Cinema. At this time the Officers were: President - Mr. A. Thirsk; Committee Members - Messrs. W.L. Baker, E. Cox, R. Dry, T. Hanson, G.T. Kirby and J.J. Fisher; Secretary - Mr. D.W. Arnold; Manager - Mr. R.E. Dixon.

By the 1960s small rural societies like Market Weighton were struggling. Rising transport costs posed a special threat to those in thinly populated areas and newly car-owning shoppers were discovering the attractions of towns like Beverley, Driffield and York with their modern cut-price stores. The Society could no longer compete and still pay a worthwhile dividend. Before 1963 was out the members agreed to give up their 60-year independence and merge with Hull & East Riding.

After the transfer, and for as long as their health allowed, Town Councillor Tom Hanson and his wife regularly travelled over to Hull for the Members' Meetings to keep an eye on how the city-based Society was looking after their business! Mrs Hanson was Secretary of the local Co-operative Women's Guild.

POCKLINGTON AND DISTRICT INDUSTRIAL CO-OPERATIVE SOCIETY LTD.

This Society was formed in 1904 and had its first registered offices at Waterloo Buildings, 15 Market Place. A 1905 Directory shows it trading in Grocery, Drapery, Boots and Shoes, Furnishing, Tailoring and Flour, the membership being 140.

In 1922 branches were operating at Bishop Wilton, Bugthorpe, Stamford Bridge and Melbourne. By 1928 the Society had developed a Bakery, Grocery Warehouse and Coal Depot in New Street, Pocklington. Another shop, at Wilberfoss, was trading by 1940.

In 1953 Mr. George Haw retired after 30 years service as Managing Secretary. The Pocklington members at first rejected the idea of a merger with Hull but as the decade wore on it was plain that fortunes were unlikely to improve by staying independent; talks reopened, leading to a merger on 29th December 1956. CRS is still represented in Pocklington with a small supermarket.

ST. ANDREW HOUSING CO-OPERATIVE LTD.

This Co-operative was formed in 1976 to try to save the small community in St. Andrew Street, Beverley, an area threatened with demolition. A study by the Hull School of Architecture showed some of the houses were capable of renovation, although others would have to be cleared. Backed by funding from the Housing Corporation, the Co-operative had successfully rehabilitated 25 houses by 1982.

To make the scheme viable new homes were then planned on the cleared sites. But, standing in the shadow of Beverley's ancient Minster, the proposed development provoked great controversy in the town. The promoters finally triumphed over two Ombudsman's reports, a High Court injunction and the demise of their main contractor, to produce a really sensitive example of the kind of community architecture favoured by the Prince of Wales.

The Co-operative owns a range of property from 4-bedroom houses to one-bedroom flats and employs a warden to support its more elderly tenants. Each tenant has a one-pound share and can vote for, and stand for election to, the Management Committee. Allocations are based on housing need but, as the Co-operative is keen to preserve the local community, many of its tenants have lived in, or been connected with, the area for a long time.

SHOEFAYRE LTD.

Readers might be surprised to learn that the Shoefayre stores in Whitefriargate, Hull and Prince Street, Bridlington are part of the Co-operative Movement. Shoefayre was formed in response to the Gaitskell Commission Report of 1958 which urged the Movement to develop multiple stores, starting in footwear. Owned jointly by the CWS and certain retail co-ops, it came to Hull in 1962 and now trades from around 320 locations nationwide.

Self-help through mutual aid: Members of Giroscope workers' Co-op pool their skills in an effort to improve the housing and employment prospects of their West Hull community.

Bridlington Co-operative Society's premises in Quay Road, circa 1906.

Premises of the former Market Weighton & District Co-operative Society. The Co-op is still represented in the town, with a modern community supermarket (Picture by courtesy of Dysons, Market Weighton).

The Hull Printers were based here in Lowgate, Hull until wartime destruction forced them to leave the city for a 'green field' site at Willerby.

With innovations such as kiosks on superstore car parks, the Co-operative Bank has made banking accessible to everyone. The austere banking halls of yesteryear deterred many people from ever opening an account.

These were the conditions

That prompted a movement

Which opened a bank

That broke the rules

But stuck to its principles

Times change but principles don't.

The concept of co-operation is alive and kicking at The Co-operative Bank.

Our commitment to provide innovative products and a quality service has been at the very root of our success.

And success brings with it greater influence.

Greater influence to support our customers' concerns about oppression, exploitation and the environment.

And while these issues are steadily finding their way onto the agendas of other organisations we can look back to those original pioneers and thank them for giving us an unfair advantage.

150 years experience in applying co-operative principles and basic values.

And attracted new customers

Who want the world to be a better place

The COOPERATIVE BANK

Why bank with one that isn't?

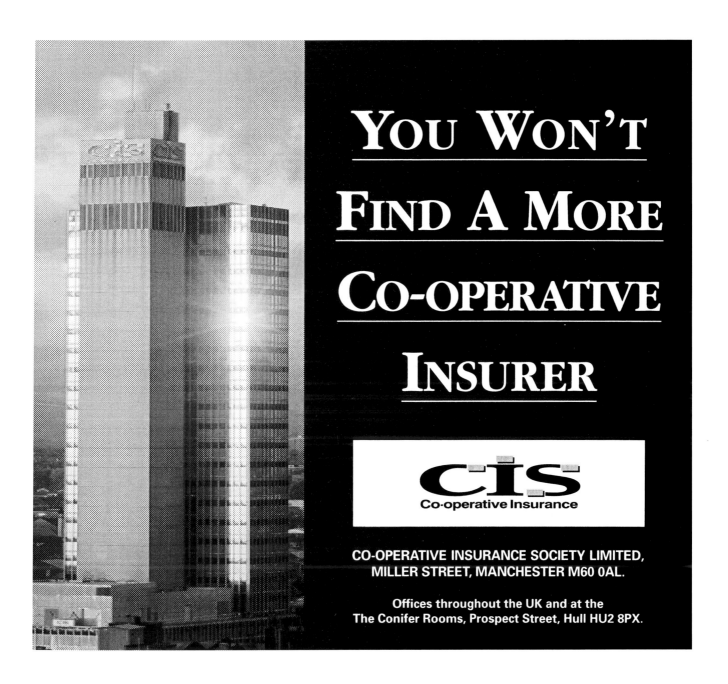

WE THINK PEOPLE ARE IMPORTANT

That's why we have more food stores serving more communities than any other retailer. That's why through our own brand products we're at the forefront of food labelling. That's why, as Britain's biggest commercial farmer, we take care of your food by using less pesticides and growing organic produce...

...and why we work with the RSPCA to help raise animal welfare standards. We think it's right to help and support the communities we serve. We've been putting your family's interests first for generations and will do so for generations to come.

We're always thinking of you.